Build a Life~giving parish

The Gift of Counsel in the Modern World

Sister Brenda Hermann, MSBT, ACSW
and Monsignor James T. Gaston, MA, STL

Liguori
LIGUORI, MISSOURI

Imprimi Potest:
Thomas D. Picton, C.Ss.R.
Provincial, Denver Province
The Redemptorists

Nihil Obstat:
The Reverend Monsignor Lawrence T. Persico, VG, JCL
Censor Liborum

Imprimatur:
The Most Reverend Lawrence E. Brandt, JCD, PhD
Bishop of Greensburg
Date: February 17, 2010

The nihil obstat and imprimatur are official declarations that a book or pamphlet is free of doctrinal or moral error. No implication is contained therein that those who have granted the nihil obstat and imprimatur agree with the contents, opinions or statements expressed.

Published by Liguori Publications
Liguori, Missouri
To order, call 800-325-9521
www.liguori.org

Library of Congress Cataloging-in-Publication Data

Hermann, Brenda.
    Build a life-giving parish : the gift of counsel in the modern world / Brenda Hermann and James T. Gaston. — 1st ed.
        p. cm.
    Includes bibliographical references.
    ISBN 978-0-7648-1891-2
    1. Parish councils. 2. Pastoral theology—Catholic Church. I. Gaston, James T. II. Title.
    BX1920.H395 2010
    254'.02—dc22

                                                                        2010006906

Liguori Publications, a nonprofit corporation, is an apostolate of the Redemptorists. To learn more about the Redemptorists, visit Redemptorists.com.

Printed in the United States of America
14 13 12 11 10   5 4 3 2 1
First edition

To the Missionary Cenacle Family,
especially the Missionary Servants
of the Most Blessed Trinity;
and to the clergy and people
of the Diocese of Greensburg, Pennsylvania.

*And he said to them, "Therefore every scribe who has been trained
for the kingdom of heaven is like the master of a household who
brings out of his treasure what is new and what is old."*

MATTHEW 13:52

Table of Contents

Preface

Sister Brenda Hermann and Monsignor James Gaston draw on their rich pastoral experiences to offer the reader exciting insights into the challenges facing pastoral councils. By drawing a line between the work of the very first church council in the Christian Scriptures to present pastoral councils, the authors raise up the value of local councils in a bold and refreshing way. Their perspective in *Build a Life-Giving Parish: The Gift of Counsel in the Modern World* is that the very mission of the pastoral council is often without consensus. Their solution is that the primary focus of a pastoral council ought to be the daily life concerns of the laity.

Build a Life-Giving Parish is full of creative notions that can prove beneficial to those who, while taking the work of the pastoral council to be a serious enterprise, also find it at times to be tedious, boring, and even unproductive. A careful analysis of the mission field of the laity, as different from that of the ordained, offers an avenue for stimulating conversation and thoughtful consideration.

This book expands the understanding of the virtue of counsel and explains how it can be used within the structure of pastoral councils in the United States. I recommend *Build a Life-Giving Parish: The Gift of Counsel in the Modern World* to clergy and laity who, together in council, seek to create a life-giving parish.

THE MOST REVEREND LAWRENCE E. BRANDT, JCD, PHD
BISHOP OF GREENSBURG
OCTOBER 2009

Foreword

If I had to give a title for the introduction of this book by Sister Brenda Hermann and Monsignor James Gaston, it would be, "I Need Your Help."

Ever since L'Arche began in 1964, when I started living with two men who had intellectual disabilities and who I had discharged from a violent and closed institution, I've been crying out, "I need your help; I need your counsel."

At that time, I knew nothing about people with disabilities except that they had no voice in society and were often treated without respect, as if they were "no persons." I had everything to learn, first of all, from them. What did they want? What did they need? Where was their pain? How do we live together, eat together, pray together? How do I give them baths and so on? I also had to learn from my mistakes and the misplaced bits of ideology that I tried to impose on these men.

Of course, I needed the help of psychiatrists. As L'Arche grew, I welcomed some men and women with severe psychological difficulties. Some were violent, some deeply depressed; some had very antisocial behavior, and others had specific psychological sickness. Yes, I needed counsel. But I also needed direct consultation with professionals in the fields of psychiatry, psychology, social services, and human behavior.

I had to learn how to work with local authorities, how to find the right sources of funding, how to run the house and then houses, and how to find the right work for people whom we had welcomed. I also needed a group of competent men and women to become the board of directors for the "trust" or the legal association I had created. As I look back, I realize how little I knew and how much I needed help with all of these entities.

After a year or so, I called a three-day meeting for all those who were collaborating with me. They were called assistants, and there were about twenty of them. I put them in three groups with a coordinator for each group. They were to answer two fundamental questions: What were the good and the not-so-good things in our life at L'Arche, and what needed changing? This was our very first council meeting.

I was astonished to find out all that was going wrong in the community. From where I stood—on my pedestal of power—everything seemed to be going fine! So we had to reorganize things. We created a community council which would meet every Thursday. I could not run things on my own; I needed counsel from others. I also had to learn how to run the council so that everyone had a voice and we could come to decisions together. L'Arche began to grow.

At every level of community, and with new communities being born, we all needed counsel. How to create L'Arche in Africa and Central America? How to become truly inculturated and not just transfer into other countries the organization and style of life that we had created in France? Maybe things worked quite well in France and Canada, but we had to learn how to live in other countries.

Fortunately, in our societies, there are men and women who are trained as "coaches." We needed them when there were difficulties in communities. We needed them to sort out what came from dysfunctional structures, what came from personality conflicts, and what came from a lack of understanding of the goals of L'Arche. To find unity, we needed help from people trained in the domain of conflict resolution. These people provided us with the technical advise we needed.

L'Arche is a community. We live together: people with disabilities and those who wish to share their lives with them. We are obviously controlled and inspected by local authorities. We are an institution inserted into a society. No one community is an island hidden away from others. We are a very human organization or institution, but we are motivated by community and spiritual goals. We don't have the answers to all our questions.

Others have lived similar things. We do not have to reinvent the wheel. This book is about seeking counsel. L'Arche now has one hundred thirty-five communities in thirty-six countries, and it is because many people have helped us on the journey. Sister Brenda Hermann has often been there to help us undo knots and show the way forward. We are all part of a growing, evolving humanity and church. We all need counsel.

This book can help us not to assume that parishes or religious communities can do it alone because they have (or think they have) the Holy Spirit and the wisdom of their tradition. In some ways, we do have the Spirit, but in other ways, we are human, terribly human. We all need help to clarify and modify dysfunctional structures that can become obstacles to the mission of the Church and the religious communities themselves. The world is evolving, needs are evolving, members of communities are evolving.

Every community needs good counsel as things change and evolve, particularly as they might hinder the clarity of the mission. They need counsel for authority to be exercised in the most fruitful way. They also need help from competent people, because communities are made up of fallible human beings.

JEAN VANIER
L'ARCHE TROSLY-BREUIL, FRANCE
SEPTEMBER 2009

Introduction

The Parish: A Community for Mission

The joys and the hopes,
the grief and the anguish
of the people of our time,
especially of those who are poor or afflicted,
are the joys and hopes,
the grief and anguish
of the followers of Christ as well.
Nothing that is genuinely human
fails to find an echo in their hearts.

GAUDIUM ET SPES 1
PASTORAL CONSTITUTION ON THE CHURCH
IN THE MODERN WORLD

At the turn of the twenty-first century, Roman Catholics are approximately 25 percent of the population of the United States. They live, work, and take leisure in every part of American culture. They are represented in every field of work, in universities, in politics, in the arts and sciences. They labor in the fields and the factories.

Catholic lay men and women design space shuttles and help their children design school projects. They give public speeches on the environment and speak with their neighbors over barbecue. They live next door to the immigrant and write national legislation.

The laity are to be leaven in society. Through their baptism, they are called to make a difference as they bring God's message of love, peace, and justice to the world.

However, their mission to the greater world is obstacle-ridden. It is a pastoral concern that many adult Catholics have not pursued faith formation beyond their earliest years of sacramental preparation. Most would admit that their ongoing faith formation comes primarily (and accidentally) through participation in the Sunday Eucharist, listening to homilies, reading the church bulletin, or searching the Internet.

Some are ambivalent about their relationship with the Church. Some may not bother going to church at all, while maintaining strong opinions about beliefs and practices. Many publicly disagree with the Church, often without having the faith formation needed to make this critique. Most adult Catholics have never read a papal encyclical or any official document on the Church's social mission in society. Where do they go to be formed in the responsibility to be the transformers of society?

The answer most often is "the parish." People shop around for a parish because they are looking for something. This "something" is often identified with good homilies, uplifting music and singing, a welcoming community, intergenerational membership with a focus on youth, and acceptance of diversity. While these needs are real, greater emphasis should be given to the wider mission of the laity when they leave the parish compound.

Today, there are more than nineteen thousand Catholic parishes in the United States. To write about the role of a pastoral council is to take into account the multiple understandings of the purpose of the parish. Parish life is influenced by many different realities. Vatican II decreed that the "whole purpose of the parish is the good of souls."[1] What is the concrete meaning of "the good of souls" today?

Vatican II's *Gaudium et Spes* beautifully articulates what the mission of the Church means to the world. This mission calls for engagement with the rapidly changing contemporary world by facilitating human interdependence, fostering marriage and family life, bringing faith to bear on culture, serving as leaven in the economic and political orders, and fostering peace and the development of the international community.

To accept *Gaudium et Spes* is to acknowledge that the mission of every parish is also to its world. The parish is to provide its members with the ideas, the practices, the experience, and the structures for participation in public and private life.

It is only a wise leader who can understand the complexity of providing pastoral care in today's reality. Wisdom and prudence are needed to equip the laity spiritually for their engagement in family and work, for taking on the political questions of the times, and for being partners in global change.

Premises

The purpose of this book is to advance theological and pastoral thinking and practice. How are we to prepare the people of God for their mission in the community and world? We begin with these premises:

~ The parish must consciously and intentionally come to see itself as THE primary formator of the laity for their role in society.
~ This way of thinking enables the parish to evaluate everything it does out of the lens of its potential to prepare the laity more effectively for their place in the world, not primarily for the parish.
~ Great (versus good) parish programs enable participants to make the necessary connections between their faith and their daily living.

~ The purpose of parish faith formation is to teach members at every age how to reflect prayerfully on the issues of their daily lives, to consider their roles in society, and to encourage them to make choices rooted in the Gospel.

~ Examples flow from the vision of *Gaudium et Spes*: How to live more simply? Foster peace even in fragmented family life? Work for quality of life for all people? Confront our overt and covert racism? Be just in our places of employment? Care about even our anonymous neighbors?, etc.

~ Homilies must be inculturated. The best homilies, people report, are those in which the homilist uses real examples that are current (not about the past) and can translate the Gospel message into practical everyday life (not pious, disembodied exhortations). Good homilies engage and challenge; they do not demean.

~ Parish community-building programs must also help members understand the need to build community in their neighborhoods and workplaces. The parish is not an escape from the challenges of family living, of being a good neighbor, or of an unhappy workplace.

~ The parish must see itself as the conduit through which God's Word is transmitted to the people who are to act upon it and go about building a more just and humane society.

~ The parish is a place where two mission fields interact: the mission field of the laity and the mission field of the ordained. In the parish setting, the ordained are to play a pivotal role in assuring that the laity are equipped and have everything necessary to "go in peace to love and serve the world."

~ When a parish operates out of this lens, those who are called to the work of council do not experience as much dissonance as the council's agenda begins to turn to what is happening in their lives or the life of the community.

~

Mary and Robert spent several months looking for a parish that would "fit" them. They had both grown up Catholic, and during their college years, neither had attended church on a regular basis. They were married in Mary's parish, but did not attend regularly until the birth of their first baby. They were searching for something that would help them make sense of some of the things happening in their world as a young family.

When asked about the criteria in helping them choose their present parish, Mary said, "Well, they have no cry room." For her, this meant that the parish would accept them bringing their children to Mass. She also went on to say that they have Liturgy of the Word for children. Robert spoke about the pastor as someone who really gave great homilies. He said, "Father used the Sunday readings to help me think about my job and the attitude I have had toward my boss. He uses good analogies, things I can understand. I have decided to talk about some of these things with a couple of other guys who are also having a hard time."

Neither Mary nor Robert has the time or energy to participate in parish programs. They do believe that their church gives them the spiritual energy they need to be parents as well as workers in their jobs. Both are called to make a difference in the world in which they live and work. This is their mission. It is the purpose of the parish, in everything it does, to remind them and to empower them for this sacred duty.

~

The quality of a parish pastoral council is directly connected to the quality of parish life and its focus, not merely within its walls, but within the wider community in which the people live. The focus of the parish's mission outward calls for an entirely new format and process of its council. This is the shift in understanding needed for the twenty-first century. This understanding of council is not new. It is a return to an age-old tradition of council operative in the Church throughout its history.

Chapter 1

Why This Book?

Pastoral Councils: A New Beginning

Pastoral councils across the United States are a magnificent testimony to the centuries-old Catholic tradition of "holding council," which began with the first-century Council of Jerusalem and continues into our own time. The tradition of council is ever ancient and ever new! In the half-century following Vatican II, much energy has been given to the implementation of councils at every level of church life. However, at the grassroots level—where the so-called "rubber hits the road"—it is no secret that we are still struggling to get it right.

The authors have experienced and pondered the struggles of councils from the perspective of both the ordained and the laity for many years. We have come to a fundamental conclusion. There is still a need for a clearer and deeper understanding of the nature and purpose of pastoral councils for both the ordained and the laity. Hence, we ask the fundamental question of when is a pastoral council really a "council"?

Veteran pastoral practitioners will remember the very first parish council meetings that were governed by Robert's Rules of Order. Discussions focused on what it meant to be a consultative group with the inevitable reminder that all decisions were to be left to the pastor. A friend once described his leadership role on the parish council then as "chairing the bored."

In the 1980s, the word "pastoral" was added to parish councils to reflect a change in canon law. This change in terminology also reflected a deepening awareness of councils as different in nature from other parish-based groups. The laity were now expected to share in the "pastoral work of the ordained," and the pastoral council was to plan for how this was to occur.

The former parish council model clearly was not working. Something else was needed. Parish planning soon became the focus of pastoral councils. This can be seen in one of the documents that was created in the Diocese of Greensburg, Pennsylvania, and which emerged within that period, entitled, "New Wine, New Wineskins." This document supported the paradigm for councils as pastoral planning bodies across the United States.

Is planning the fundamental purpose of a council? Our experiences suggest that it is not.

We believe that over the centuries, inherent in the tradition of council is a deep and abiding belief in the Holy Spirit's guidance of the people of God. This guidance is manifest when laity and the ordained reflect together on the signs of the times and respond to these signs within any given culture.

Christ's mission given to the Church is to bring God's love into the world. Through this evangelizing action, there is an element of transformation both within one's culture and within oneself. Transformation occurs as we go deeper into understanding God's Word as it is to be lived in the circumstances before us.

Where is our world in need of God's love today? Who is responsible to bring this love into society? Of course, we know the answer: We all are responsible! This answer begs another question: How are we to do this? The answer to this question leads to the basic premise of our book. What is the purpose of a pastoral council? We will answer with these words: "taking counsel in council."

We begin by defining two basic concepts: the mission field of the laity and the mission field of the ordained.

Field of Mission: The Laity

In a meeting with a parish council in the mid 1980s, a discussion took place about "helping Father in the parish." The laity was very animated about trying to develop a plan for the parish building project. They were very involved in evaluating parish programs, thinking about the new school year, and anticipating the parish school's expansion.

During council members' conversations at lunch, there was little discussion of the parish's concerns. Rather the parents present were focused on the concerns of their children. Some families were confronted with serious financial problems. There were a myriad of other issues as well, including aging and ill parents, marital breakups, and unemployed family members. None of these daily life concerns were considered "pastoral" and brought to the table of council. Council conversations focused on internal parish programs, facilities, and activities.

In the intervening twenty-five years, some things have not changed in the vision and work of councils despite new theories, processes, and structures that have been developed.

We came to an insight that has only grown over these twenty-five years. The daily life concerns of the laity are indeed the primary pastoral concerns of the Church. As such, these concerns must be the subject of the work of pastoral councils.

We use the phrase "taking counsel in council" to describe the deliberate process of listening, dialogue, deciding, and implementing pastoral responses for God's people.

These everyday issues constitute the "mission field" of the laity. It is within these daily circumstances that the baptized are called to receive and bring God's love. Indeed, this is where the laity are to be pastored and helped to become missionaries to others.

Field of Mission: The Ordained

In 2002, a pastor related feeling overwhelmed by the complex pastoral needs and issues of the people. Because of numerous parish closings within the diocese, he was now the sole priest in a congregation of more than two thousand families. He was able to hire a sufficient number of staff members to assure that programs and volunteers were supervised. At the same time, many things affected the community in which the parish was located. He stated that expectations of him from the diocese had increased, mostly due to the ever changing nature of diocesan priorities.

He began to question himself and his pastoral effectiveness, especially in preaching. "I just feel so disconnected from peoples' lives," he stated. When pressed further on this, it was clear that he really did have a sense of the issues in peoples' lives through his pastoral visits, through stopping to chat with people in a variety of settings, and through the stories of the staff. "But," he said, "there is no place to put these concerns, no place for deepening my understanding of these pastoral concerns with my parishioners."

When asked about his pastoral council, he explained that they did a great job helping him develop a yearly plan with goals and objectives. He described how these goals and objectives are reached, explaining that every program was evaluated by the council and new goals were created. However, he explained, there was no time to really talk about issues in peoples' lives as the council meetings were already too long, and people were very busy. He could only state that the parish had "a lot of programs." In his own way, he was articulating some of the major concerns in his field of mission as a priest.

The mission field of the ordained is where and how they represent and render Christ visible in the midst of the people they shepherd. The priest strikes a pastoral relationship *(in persona Christi)* with his people. He is not there simply to perform religious duties or functions. Nor is he there merely to administer the parish's temporal goods or to assure a smooth running operation. All of these administrative functions are important in parish or diocesan life, but most of those can be delegated to laity working within Church ministry. The unique role of the ordained in the liturgy, in sacramental life, in preaching, and in pastoral care (his field of mission) has a different focus than the mission field of the laity.

Effective pastoral leadership requires attentiveness to these daily life issues and concerns of the people of God, for their joys and their sorrows are the subject of the mission of the Church as lived out in a faith community.

Council: The Intersection of Two Mission Fields

With these two stories we lay the foundation for what we have come to believe is the essential role of council. The purpose of council is to convene the ordained and laity, to give and take counsel on the critical issues of the people of God that require a pastoral response. This is the parish's perennial mission. Pastoral leaders must always ask: "How are the people to receive pastoral care effectively in this place and in this time?"

Authentic counsel is given when the two distinct and different perspectives of the ordained and the laity are brought into dialogue for the sake of this pastoral mission. Council is the forum and the time-tested structure. Counsel is the gift offered and clarified in the continuing dialogue that occurs. The ultimate goal of the process is to discern, within the limits of the possible, what is God's will for the people in the daily circumstances of their lives. There is no other arena within a parish where these deliberations can occur properly or strategically—staff meetings, focus groups, and all other discussions notwithstanding.

The table of council is the place where the distinct mission fields of the laity and the ordained formally intersect, each sharing its unique experience of and insight into the joys and sorrows of the people of God. These joys and sorrows correlate with the signs of the times. They usually exist not just within the parish, but as part of the broader community or culture. These realities must be pondered and better understood. The signs of the times signal the hungers of the people crying out for God's abiding love and care. Pastoral leadership must hear these cries, determine what response(s) are required, and ultimately act courageously

to support and strengthen them to take up their mission each day.

The pastoral council does not exist to make a better parish. Rather, it is the place where the will of God is discovered for the community in which its members live and work. The pastoral council exists to develop a stronger sense of mission in its entire people. To the degree that this occurs, a better parish is inevitable.

Guided by the wisdom of the Holy Spirit in council, the ordained and the laity take counsel from one other. Counsel focuses on such questions as:

~ How is God's love to be brought to the pastoral concerns emerging in the lives of the people of this community?
~ How are we to respond as parish community?
~ What is God revealing to us and asking of us at this time in our history?
~ What challenging pastoral responses may require courage and fortitude of us as a council? Or of the pastor as leader?

Taking counsel in council is not an easy task. The fields of mission of the ordained and the laity are inherently polar opposites, yet both are profoundly important to the life of the Church. Council is like the fulcrum of the seesaw. It holds in balance both mission fields.

To take counsel, the ordained and the laity must develop a deeper understanding of their particular field of mission. Each must understand the mission field of the other and the complementary relationship that exists between them. Such understanding is the foundation for taking counsel.

Laity often complain that the ordained do not appreciate their stress in coping with family and work concerns. Similarly, many clergy would admit that the laity do not fully grasp the breadth and depth of their pastoral concerns. Who would know how diverse are the tasks and responsibilities that fill the average day of a pastor? Or their stresses in ministering within a society that can be selective in accepting Church teachings?

Some laity find the Church irrelevant and often feel that the ordained preach and minister to a world other than their own. Others believe that the Church or parish is less concerned about the daily concerns of people and more focused on enforcing doctrine and Church regulations. Our experience suggests that increasing numbers of Catholics are becoming more selective in choosing a place of worship, establishing parish affiliation, or taking on personal or family religious commitments.

The ordained seek to articulate a Gospel message clearly and in support of the laity's role in marriage and family, in the workplace, and in the political and social arena. They are not always sure how to do this effectively in a society that is deeply polarized or that easily misinterprets the teachings of the Church. How, therefore, are they to exercise their role as pastors in a meaningful and fruitful way?

Taking counsel in council is critical in determining what and how to provide relevant pastoral care. We would like to think that if the Church had not invented council almost 2000 years ago, we would have to do it today. Benjamin Franklin is purported to have said, "Those who won't be counseled cannot be helped." So we ask, "Is there anyone among us today who does not need help?"

In the chapters that follow, we will explore several key themes and offer concrete suggestions for transitioning pastoral councils from functioning as planning groups back to the long and deep Church tradition of taking counsel in council. These themes include:

1. Exploring the mission field of the laity and briefly discussing the emergence of lay ministry in the Church in the United States. We pose the question: In what does lay holiness consist?

2. Developing the mission field of the ordained and examining some obstacles to their taking counsel and the exercising of effective pastoral leadership.

3. Describing how a *counsel in council* meeting might look.

4. Outlining the spiritual practices used in councils: *faith sharing, pastoral reflection, discernment,* and *theological reflection.*

5. Examining the virtues of *prudence, wisdom, counsel,* and *fortitude* as essential elements of taking counsel in council.

6. Addressing the formation that is necessary for entering into the dialogue of council.

7. Reflecting on the life of Father Thomas Augustine Judge, CM, founder of the Missionary Cenacle Family in the United States, in 1909. He serves as a model of "thinking with the Church" in an era when the laity could not be considered as missionaries, and before council was considered essential to local church life.

8. Throughout the book, we will share some of our personal experiences and our convictions about the need to return to counsel in council in the Church.

Chapter 2

The Mission Field of the Laity

The Meaning of Mission and Field of Mission

In Baltimore City, on the wall of a local car wash, hangs a rather large framed document entitled, "Our Mission Statement." Why would a car wash need a statement of mission? When asked, the owner indicated that he was very serious about pleasing the customers through the cleaning service he provided. He stated proudly that when he looked at the framed mission statement each day (who could miss it!), he was reminded again of why he was in business: "It is about the customer...the customer!" he said.

It seems everywhere one goes today, from hospitals to churches, to schools and nonprofit groups, a mission statement hangs on the wall. Sometimes there are flowers, statues, candles, or other decorations around it. Mission statements serve as reminders why an institution exists and, in some cases, a reminder of what the founder envisioned for the company or service. Clearly, having a public statement of mission is very important in today's developed world.

Remember the 1986 film, *The Mission*, or the TV series turned movie, *Mission Impossible?* While fundamentally very different films, each of them in its title reinforced the fundamental concept of having a statement of mission and also showed what it meant to be actively involved in that mission in the field, even if considered "impossible" to the viewers.

What do we mean by mission, and what is its field? If Jesus were to have framed and posted his mission statement on the wall, it could be found in Luke 4:18–19:

> *The Spirit of the Lord is upon me, because he has anointed me to bring good news to the poor. He has sent me to proclaim release to the captives and recovery of sight to the blind, to let the oppressed go free, to proclaim the year of the Lord's favor.*

In these words, Jesus makes clear that his mission, given to him by his Father, is to reveal God's unending love and mercy for all humankind to every corner of the earth. This unconditional love is to be shared in very practical ways, in works of mercy and justice toward my neighbor, and in ensuring that this good news is shared with the poor. In other words, the entire human family—with a special emphasis on the disenfranchised—is the recipient (customer) of this mission!

Jesus did not die without a backup plan. We know that this plan included an ordinary crew of men and women who were empowered by the Holy Spirit to continue this mission. They had to determine the ways and means of bringing God's love to others within the confines of their culture and history. This mission continues within the cultures of today. This is the pastoral mission of the Church, which is carried out by all the baptized from generation to generation. The mission does not change. God's love is never ending.

However, the circumstances of today are different from those of the time of Christ. How are we to live and experience this pastoral mission in the circumstances of today? How are the people of God in New York City to live the mission differently than the people of God in Seattle, Washington? Each of these places is its own unique "field of mission."

Field of mission, as we use it, refers to the place and the circumstances of everyday life where each of us is called to be. Each place, each circumstance, presents us with the opportunity to bring God's love (the mission) to it. Some opportunities are wonderful "mountain top experiences." Other times may require a form of tough love, but we are never excused from thinking of the recipient, the customer. It is within our field of mission that we are sanctified and the Gospel message is shared.

As we explore "counsel in council," it is important to grasp this fundamental principle of mission. The Church exists to carry on the mission of Jesus. The Church as an institution in society may need buildings and properties, but only to the degree that each serves this mission. The local Church (first the diocese, then the parish) serves as the place of witness for the community of believers. The Church's assets, buildings, and structures exist within a community of people who live their daily lives in another mission field, that of the laity.

The Mission at the Doorstep

Every morning millions of people get out of bed and go *to* something. Many choose to stay home and are involved in raising children or caring for aging family members. There are, of course, increasing numbers in the ranks of the retired. They are likely to describe their daily lives as uneventful. They are of every race and creed, every ethnic and religious group. They are young and old, rich and poor, married and not. They are civic, business, and political leaders.

The universal desire of all of people is to be happy and to be loved. This desire is not the "Hollywood" type of happiness, but that which is experienced among family and friends: the gift of acceptance and peace. Happiness embraces, for example, parents' hope that their children will have enough to eat, that they will receive an adequate education, that they will have opportunities to grow and prosper, and that as they grow older, they will be treated with respect and be blessed ultimately with a "happy death."

However, happiness is elusive. We suffer, we are at war, we endure famine, violence, and injustice. We live in an imperfect world, and we are painfully aware of the absence of happiness in so much of life.

In short, the laity's field of mission is our broken and violent world. It is a gigantic mission field and is always ripe for receiving a message of hope. It is into this reality, this field of mission, that the baptized faithful are to bring God's message of love.

The laity who live and work in the midst of society and culture are often its best translators and interpreters. Their experiences, often unprocessed, must be articulated and heard by those who seek to minister to them.

Catholic social teaching declares that the laity are called to transform society. They are the ones who are to speak to the injustices of everyday life (in the picket line and at the check-out counter), to feed the hungry, (at the food bank and at the family table), to visit the sick (participate in the *Race for the Cure* and check in on the elderly neighbor across the street), to clothe the naked (support the clothing drive and care for the new baby), and to visit those in prison (advocate for prison reform and provide some relief to a person with a mentally ill spouse).

All are empowered to do this through their baptism. Whatever they do and wherever they go, they are presented with innumerable opportunities to bring this message of God's love into their world, not so much by their formal ministries, but in their daily routines. They represent the love of Christ.

Laity are missionaries through their baptism. They may never leave the country, but they are still in mission and this mission takes place within the providence of their everyday lives. They are on mission most often without formal training or degrees in theology or ministry. Some of the greatest missionaries have never left their home towns. Some have even been illiterate or without any formal education.

~

"Miss Sally," as she is known to her neighbors, is a wonderful cook. Her chicken and biscuits are to die for! Once a week, Miss Sally cooks up a huge batch and invites the elderly widowers of the community to come and have lunch with her. Each of them shows up with a container to take some home. After the meal, she listens to them to see if there is anything else she can do. It was very edifying to see these grateful, lonely, elderly men get a good meal, plus some to go. When a remark was made about her good works, Miss Sally replied: "Oh don't be foolish; everybody wants to be a good neighbor. This is not anything! I just love to cook."

If Miss Sally were asked if she was holy, she would probably say "no." She would probably say that Mother Teresa is holy, but that she herself didn't qualify. Yet, she sought out the unmet need and used her gifts to respond. Isn't that love and holiness in action?

~

How often have we heard the disbelief of the laity in their own holiness? They still believe that theirs is a "lesser" life than the ordained or those in religious life. Old convictions die hard. Laity are reluctant to believe that their call to heroic sanctity is lived out as they engage the challenges in their marriages, at work, in raising their families, coping with illness and injustice, facing financial stress, contending with difficulties in their neighborhoods. Their faith is operative and tested in each of these life situations.

~

During a workshop, a pastor asked his people to think quietly about all the holy people in their world and to name them. When he asked for the response, over 98% named people of heroic stature such as Pope John Paul II and Mother Teresa. One person said, "You are holy, Father, because you are a priest." Another person responded, "My mother." When the priest asked why she mentioned her mother, the woman responded by identifying all her mom's beautiful qualities. When he asked if anyone named themselves, the audience fell silent. He then asked them if they ever practiced patience or extended forgiveness. Did they pray? Did they try to be faithful in their love for each other? His intention was to help them realize that their call to holiness is within these everyday actions, even though they are not perfect.

~

The holiness of the laity, their participation in the life of divine love, is directly related to life in their mission field. They do not have to leave family and friends to pursue holiness. The laity are in places where no one else will ever be. This is their unique and powerful place of mission.

Few people realize that their holiness is imbedded in dealing with these realities of their daily lives. Unfortunately, they rarely hear this truth articulated in the parish. The often unspoken message is that the lay person's involvement in parish ministry as a eucharistic minister or a lector (a ministry near the altar or "at the parish") gives them more of the halo than being a mom or dad taking care of an ill child. The things done in the remaining twenty-three hours apart from Sunday Mass do not seem to count.

Some of the laity work more directly in addressing the larger issues of contemporary society, especially at a global or national level. Some are involved in the work for peace and justice. Some are in places of danger or high risk work. Many are in the military or in service to their country in other ways. This is their providence. This is where their holiness is expressed and purified.

While the majority of the laity may never come to the parish's table of council themselves, those who give counsel in council must remember that all are members of the faith community and that they need to be equipped to be missionaries in their daily life and work.

As the laity come to fuller appreciation of the holiness that is theirs and understand that they are missionaries in the providence of their daily lives, they will come to fuller participation at the table of council. Their role in council is not primarily shaped by any specific theological training they may have received, but in their capacity to be the interpreters of their own reality, their own providence. True counsel cannot be taken without their participation in the dialogue. This dialogue can only be done effectively over time and requires deep mutual respect between the laity and the ordained.

Lay Ecclesial Ministry
and the Field of Mission

The field of mission of the laity should not be confused with the various forms of onsite parish-based ministries nor lay ecclesial ministries that are emerging in the Church. In *Evangelium Nuntiandi* 11, Pope Paul VI describes the ministry of the lay faithful within the Church: "The laity can also feel called, or be called, to cooperate with their pastors in the service of the ecclesial community, for the sake of its growth and life. This can be done through the exercise of different kinds of ministries according to the grace and charisms which the Lord has been pleased to bestow on them."

Within the last four decades, the laity have become essential to the variety of formal ministries conducted in the name of the Church. It is the laity who teach the faith to young children, as well as to adults. They are the people working in soup kitchens and shelters. They work in justice networks, run marriage programs, retreat centers, offer marriage counseling, bereavement, and other such actions in the name of the parish community. Some have formal staff positions in the parish and can serve as business managers, coordinators of ministry, and lay pastoral associates. Serving on a parish pastoral council is also a form of lay ministry. There are thousands of lay men and women who volunteer in their parish and fulfill roles of service and outreach. Lay volunteers are the backbone of most parish services.

Often the work of the laity is beyond the local parish community in other church institutions and or diocesan offices. Laity can be chancellors and canon lawyers. Some are theologians and experts in Church history and doctrine. Many are the directors of the social services of the diocese. In some cases, laity are administrators of parishes without a resident pastor. Increasingly, we see an educated laity taking on positions of authority and prominence in Church structures.

The laity who serve in official ecclesial ministries are expected to be competent. Across the United States, dioceses have developed lay formation or education programs. Some of the roles in ecclesial ministry demand a formal degree or a higher education.

Are the laity who work in the Church on the fast track to holiness more so than their peers who work at the local pizza shop? Maybe, but if so, it is not based on the fact that they work for the Church! Saint Teresa of Avila says it quite clearly: "God walks amid the pots and the pans."

All are called to holiness. Holiness is the gift of God. We become holy through our graced response to God in bringing our unique gifts to bear in the concrete opportunities given to us over a lifetime grace. Each of us has a call, a vocation—and the gifts and the grace to live this out.

While there is a great awareness and acceptance of laity in lay and ecclesial ministries, the fundamental truth remains that the primary mission field of the laity is NOT within the Church itself, but within family and society. It is here that most will be called to holiness. These are the voices that are critical for taking counsel in council.

At daybreak he departed and went into a deserted place. And the crowds were looking for him; and when they reached him, they wanted to prevent him from leaving them. But he said to them, "I must proclaim the good news of the kingdom of God to the other cities also; for I was sent for this purpose.

LUKE 4:42-43

Chapter 3

The mission field of the ordained

The Mission Field and Daily Life of the Ordained

The mission field of the ordained—as the primary collaborators of the diocesan bishop—is to oversee the concrete mission of transmitting God's abiding love revealed in Jesus Christ to the people of the community they serve.

It was one of the great pleasures of life to have met and worked with the late Monsignor Joseph Gremillion of Louisiana. He died August 9, 1994, leaving behind a legacy of great work including his contribution to the Notre Dame Study of Catholic Parish Life. Joe, as he was fondly called, was a priest whose field of mission took him to a southern parish in the 1950s, to Catholic Relief Services, to the Pontifical Commission for Peace and Justice, and, in 1974, to become an adjunct professor at Notre Dame. He was a brilliant and articulate man.

What was most remarkable about Joe, however, were not his notable achievements. "No," he would say, "it was the years I spent as a simple country pastor in a white parish in the midst of a black community that shaped my sense of mission and ministry." Joe once said that it was his parish experience that ignited his passion for peace and justice. It was his formative experience and he sought to remain, at heart, a simple southern pastor. Those of us who knew him believed it.

What does it mean to be formed concretely as a priest for mission and ministry, and how is this accomplished in his field of mission?

In 2008, the National Catholic Education Association Seminary Department published an assessment tool for seminaries. Of the nine ministerial duties and tasks of a Catholic priest that are listed, two relate to personal development. The remaining seven could well describe the priest's "mission field," in which he celebrates liturgy and sacraments, provides pastoral care and spiritual guidance, teaches the faith, leads parish administration, practices a ministry of presence with parish groups, participates in the life of the diocesan Church, and engages with diverse publics.[1]

The way in which a priest operates in his mission field is a function of the pastoral relationship he strikes with the people. The mission of the ordained is not simply to perform the religious or sacramental functions that flow from Holy Orders. They are to establish the right relationship, *in persona Christi*, with the people in service to their journey to God.

The ordained are the bearers of two sometimes contradictory roles that carry both spiritual and hierarchal authority. They live a paradox. In Catholic teaching, the pastor is the locus of legitimate authority in the parish. Yet at the same time, he is among the people and is to be their servant leader. Real religious authority is intensely personal and ultimately social.

The ordained do not go out to other jobs in society as do the laity. Their pastoral task is to shepherd the people by keeping in touch with their daily life concerns to help them bridge these concerns as they affect their relationship with God. Their canonical role as pastors is authoritative of itself.

However, effective pastoral leadership requires attentiveness to the daily life issues and concerns of the people of God, for their joys and sorrows are the subject of the Church's mission. In this sense, mission and ministry cannot be exercised "in general," but rather "in specific"—relevant to the unique problems and challenges that people cannot avoid every day.

How is this listening or attentiveness to occur for the ordained? It occurs in many one-on-one encounters, in attendance at meetings, in following the news media, in reading and reflecting, in personal and liturgical prayer, and by participating in civic and diocesan life. Much of this is accomplished indirectly and informally. This is the mission field of the ordained.

The United States Bishops' document on preaching, *Fulfilled in Your Hearing*, affirms that the preacher's attentiveness in listening to the joys and the sorrows of the people enables him to identify with his hearers. He is encouraged to "connect the dots" between the lives of the people and the meaning of the Gospel. This skill demands that he is first a listener before he is a speaker. It also requires the openness (intention) and the skill (capacity) of reflecting on the meaning of events of peoples' daily lives, as well as his own.

This role of listener can and should also be applied to the ordained in his daily field of mission. He is to be the great connector. He is to help people find and articulate meaning in their lives, even when it is difficult to find it within his own.

The ordained person lives out his mission in a way far different from the laity. His growth in holiness and his developing spirituality are connected to and expressed in his pastoral ministry. He grows in the pastoral role as the people allow him to function in this way. He comes to appreciate the laity's "field of mission" by entering more deeply into the joys and sorrows of others regularly—often going from funeral to wedding to baptism within twenty-four hours. He is to help people find forgiveness and to make sense of their brokenness, their grief and their sorrow. He visits the sick, prays with the dying, comforts the young and the old. At times he is weary and not always up to his game. Not infrequently, he is the recipient of someone's unresolved anger at God, at the Church, or at life itself. In his vocation, he can have unreal expectations thrust upon him from different directions—along with those he may place upon himself. Such issues should be addressed in continuing clergy education and formation programs.

In his field of mission, the ordained person walks, talks, and interacts with the laity. In this continuing dialogue, the laity help to shape him mentally and spirituality. They love him, forgive him, but they also challenge him. He is to seek their counsel about how they together are to live out the pastoral mission in this time and space, this culture and community.

The field of mission is ever changing. The realities of today are different from even twenty years ago. Neither the growth of lay ecclesial ministries nor of the diaconate provides a full solution to the unending pastoral needs of people. These specific ministries do not replace the fundamental role of all the baptized who themselves are to bring God's love and healing into every corner of their world. This is the primary role of all the laity, not simply the few who take on roles in Church ministry. None of these, of course, can replace the unique role of the ordained in the faith community.

To know what to do and how to shepherd God's people, the ordained cannot afford to ignore the essential wisdom of the people to whom he ministers. We contend that the people too must participate with him, and he with them, in determining how pastoral care is to be given and who is best gifted to do it.

This exchange is the core of taking counsel. It acknowledges that the gifts of laity and ordained are distinct but complimentary. The pastoral mission of the Church requires both.

What makes taking counsel so difficult for some of the ordained? Why do some refuse to have pastoral councils? The following are some of the challenges leaders must face.

Pastoral Leadership Challenges Today

When listening and working with pastors, two things emerge: their sense of their call to pastor God's people and their sense of the changing times. Some admit feeling inadequate because of the rapidity of change. Some just believe that due to such circumstances as age, health, additional assignments, and general morale today, they find it difficult to keep up with the demands placed upon them. Some simply are choosing not to change.

Beyond internal ecclesial concerns, the mission field of the ordained is complicated by several challenges that all those in any leadership role face in today's culture. We briefly touch on the following challenges.

Relativism

Relativism appears in various forms and messages today: "There is no objective, absolute truth." "Truth is what you believe it to be; something can be true for you but not for me." Freedom of choice is highly prized in our consumer society. Choice extends to value systems, beliefs, and lifestyle choices; all are seen as equally valid. Choice of religious belief is often eclectic, by "mix and match," or whatever allows one to feel comfortable or meets an immediate need.

The exercise of authority and leadership is challenged by the chaos and relativism of the postmodern era. If everything is important or nothing is important, how is one to continue? For example, there are many pastoral challenges in ministering to engaged couples. How should a parish minister to this group? What are their beliefs and practices regarding sexuality? What influences their understanding and expectations of intimacy in their relationships? What are the critical issues (joys and sorrows) that young adults face in their relationships today? How is this different from a generation ago? How does their faith support or interfere with their growth towards integrity and maturity?

It is a great temptation for a pastor to pass judgment on engaged couples (usually negatively), especially when they are living in nontraditional ways. Much of this is foreign to the experience and formation of the ordained. What is required to engage in conversations with them about these issues, to provide them with deeper spiritual formation in Church teaching on these matters? Sadly, without a grasp of the chaos or relativism in the lives of young adults today, the pastoral care of engaged couples can easily be reduced to lectures, demands, procedures, and marriage forms. What wisdom and pastoral response is required here and how is it acquired?

~

A priest who spent time developing a Theology on Tap ministry in the area came to an unexpected conclusion. His original intent was to sponsor lectures on topics of interest to the Church. In planning sessions with young adult leaders, it became clear to him that their "burning issues" and priorities needed to be aired and understood before they would even consider listening to lectures on doctrinal or religious topics.

When the pastor sought counsel with his pastoral council about this matter, one of the first suggestions from a member was to arrange focus groups with young adults to discuss these issues.

It took some time and a challenge from the pastor to convince the council members that they already possessed a great deal of knowledge and experience with young adults since many of them had children in this age group.

As the dialogue ensued, it became apparent that there was much more wisdom in the group's lived experience with their adult children from which to draw "counsel in council." Out of the wisdom culled in council, the parish was able to develop a more focused and relevant Theology on Tap process for its members.

Instant Communication and Changing Technology

Twitter, Facebook, Google, Bing, MySpace, Safari, Web sites, Yahoo, and blogs are but a few of the endless words used in the language of instant communication. Today, we don't just have a phone; we have a smart phone! Buying a new TV takes a certain amount of technical intelligence to decipher the choices. We no longer use a VCR; we use Blu-ray. Such is the rapidity of change.

~

A middle-aged pastor related the story about a teenage parishioner using her cell phone during his homily. When asked why the young woman was using it during Mass, she replied that she was "tweeting" her friends and letting them know that she was in church. "I told them that your homily was pretty good," she told him, "and they sent me a tweet saying that they were jealous because their homily is so boring!"

The pastor related that he did not have a clue what she was talking about. He could see her fingers moving very rapidly and assumed that putting that much energy into a gadget meant that she was not paying attention.

~

Is that true? Perhaps this was her way of paying attention in today's world of instant communication. No, we are not advocating that people use Twitter during Mass. Rather, we are pointing out the difference in thinking from generation to generation in a time of change and rapid new technology. A pastor can feel intimidated and embarrassed at not knowing or being able to stay current on how to use the latest technology.

Not all pastors relate to the frustration in the use of newer technology, and many have found it to be exciting and challenging. "How," one asked, "can we use it better in the pastoral work before us?" We would add, how can it assist in the taking of counsel?

Unrealistic Leader Expectations

This applies to expectations of self as well as a group's expectations of the person who comes into leadership. It is impossible for leaders to anticipate the expectations that can and will be placed on them before assuming the role. Leaders must enter this painful, liminal space alone; they must be disabused of the fantasies induced either by their idealized beliefs or by their need to please or to cater to those who placed them in office.

This becomes a critical challenge in parish life as the numbers of available clergy continue to decrease in dioceses. There is still a lag among the laity who, even knowing the limits of the pastor, expect instant access and response from him when an emergency occurs.

Misunderstanding Church Culture

How often have we heard that the Church is not a democracy? It has its own distinct values, concerns, and style of governance. These realities are often foreign to even the most churched lay people who live in a world of best practices, evaluations, "appreciative inquiry," bonuses, merit pay, layoffs, pink slips, and brain dumps. Corporations have a governing board of directors and a CEO or CFO. This does not automatically translate into church life. Ask any lay person who has left the world of business to work within church structures. Some things may correspond; many things do not. The cultures are diverse. Not everything transfers from the corporate culture to church life and culture.

Business can offer the Church unique insights into management and leadership. However good they may be, business models cannot simply be applied to the model of pastoral leadership needed in the Church. Grave mistakes can be made when a pastor lacks any business acumen or if he sees administration as his main role to the neglect of the pastoral needs of the people. Care must be taken when, to help the pastor, laity are hired from business and industry without appreciation of the unique culture of the "business of the Church."

The ordained are missioned as "shepherds of the flock." Pastors are to be shepherds of the people. Effective pastoring, however, requires establishing the right relationship with people, knowing them in their life circumstances. Learning to be a pastor is a "time sensitive" activity. It is easy for the ordained at all levels to lose touch with the grass roots. The challenge is to stay connected. Thus the questions: What model of pastoral leadership do the ordained need today? What model must develop in times of rapid and major changes, for example, when society is in a recession? When the people of God enjoy prosperity? When people age? In times of war?

Autocratic Leadership

No pastor wants to admit to being an autocrat. Why would an autocrat have difficulty in taking counsel? By definition, an autocrat is someone who insists on complete obedience from his or her followers. Such a leader is a person who has absolute power over the organization or group. The rules are often such that followers give this type of authority to the person. At its worst, this can result in a form of people's learned helplessness over their lives and the direction of their future.

Once becoming engaged in church ministries, including the ministry of council, many Catholics soon feel disempowered by negative experiences with the hierarchical use of authority in church settings. At its worst, church life can appear highly autocratic. Very often, laity are resigned to the fact that their input is relativized by the priorities and agenda of the ordained. If this is the case, it is almost a given that their invitation to "giving counsel" in a new setting would be viewed with suspicion and sarcasm.

In the past, when the ordained were the most educated and the only ones schooled in theology and Church law, autocratic styles of leadership were often accepted as the norm. This paralleled the use of authority in the wider community. People today are more sophisticated, more cosmopolitan, more egalitarian, and therefore highly resentful of any impression given that they are to be "rubber stamps" for any unilateral agenda. In this context, autocracy is contrary to council.

The ordained must take care to monitor their personal agendas in leadership and council. There can be many subtle forces that can contribute to becoming excessively autocratic in leadership. We have seen this in the following behaviors and scenarios:

~ The ordained leader automatically believes that he "knows" more than the laity, especially about the Church. The laity allow this perception to continue when they are unclear about their own identity as the people of God and their role in the mission of the Church.

~ The ordained leader experiences trepidation or ambivalence and has the need to mask this fear in bravado. This trepidation is often connected to the resistance to change or the embarrassment at having to ask for assistance.

~ The ordained leader exerts pressure to focus on results rather than process during a time of organizational chaos or change. This can be connected to a belief that one can control the outcomes merely through action steps. Impatience or lack of interest in "process" makes the taking of counsel impossible.

~ The ordained leader continually succumbs to time and financial constraints. These become the bottom line and primary criteria for evaluation of every activity.

~ The ordained leader operates out of an inordinate need to please, to be well thought of, or to fulfill the expectations of others such as critics, higher authority, financial supporters, or other people of influence. This fundamental flaw will prevent him from making difficult decisions when he fears rejection.

~ The ordained leader operates with unconscious biases or generalizations from personal experience which can impede openness. ("One parish is just like any other.")

~ The ordained leader is driven by fears of failure, inadequacy, intimidation, or conflict. These can immobilize a leader and no action will be forthcoming.

There are, of course, moments when deliberative leadership is a necessity. One of these might be when direction is needed, especially in urgent situations. A wise and prudent pastoral leader will use this method only rarely. It should also be clear that there are situations where consensus is NOT appropriate or even desired.

There is a critical difference between being an autocrat and having the authority to make the final decision. Clearly, the ordained leader as pastor has an authority in Church life not reserved for the laity. While he may at times have to make a decision contrary to a council's counsel, it should never be done lightly, nor without an appropriate explanation of the logic underlying the decision. Taking counsel in council requires attentiveness to these realities.

When the ordained leader is clear on his field of mission, has an awareness of his own strengths and weaknesses, and understands mission as primary, he will be more open to taking counsel with the laity. These deliberations will not be primarily about making a better parish, but about how the parish and its members can make their world a better place, in the image of God's kingdom.

Chapter 4

The goal of council: improving pastoral care

What Is Pastoral Care?

One summer, while driving through France and approaching Mont San-Michel, a group of us saw an overwhelmingly beautiful sight of sheep grazing in the verdant fields. It was a truly pastoral sight. As we drove along, however, we never saw a shepherd, at least in the way shepherds are most often described. Instead we saw farm equipment and various types of workers in the field.

When is the last time you saw a shepherd tending a flock of sheep? Outside of pictures, most of us might live our entire lives without ever meeting a real, live shepherd, yet we use the language of "pastoral" all the time!

We use the word *pastoral* to describe the lifestyle of shepherds whose task it is to move sheep from one location to another. The imagery of Jesus as the Good Shepherd is both powerful and moving to those who pray for his protection and guidance.

In ecclesial circles, the word pastoral is used to describe the mission of the Church. In pastoral theology, the word refers to practical ways of ministering to God's people. The Church's pastoral mission is to facilitate this holy enterprise under the guidance of the Holy Spirit. The call and grace given in baptism is to grow in holiness and to participate in this mission in daily life.

Pastoral care also includes the sacramental ministry provided by a priest. It can be applied to the ways in which the clergy and the laity care for one another in the name of Christ.

~

Dave, a young energetic family man, went skiing with a group of friends. His wife and family gave him the trip as a gift because he worked so hard to support and care for them. During this weekend, Dave was seriously injured and was paralyzed from the neck down. It was devastating for him and for his family. Josie was a stay-at-home mom with three young children. The family needed financial and social services, but they also needed the pastoral care of the priest and the parishioners.

Dave's pastor was one of the first persons called when Dave had his accident. It did not take him long to see that this family needed a tremendous amount of support. Within a week, one of the parishioners organized twelve different families to provide meals and care on a rotating basis. Others looked into ways of providing financial support to help the family get through the emergency. Much of this support continues until today, although some of the services have been modified.

~

This illustrates how pastoral care is provided in a complementary way by both the ordained and laity within a parish. In the daily life of people, pastoral care is expressed in such simple ways as welcoming, listening, supporting, encouraging, offering hospitality, providing a service, giving financial support, and befriending.

The wise pastoral leader today understands the complexity of providing pastoral care. This leader also understands the complexity of providing the laity with the spiritual support and resources to live and work in a complex society.

Before pastoral care can be given, the question is, "Pastoral care for what?" How are the laity to be equipped spiritually for their pastoral engagement in the daily concerns of family, at work, in knowing and caring for their neighbors, in properly connecting faith with the political questions of the day, and in being partners in a global world?

While the vocation of the ordained is to assure that the laity have everything they need to fulfill this role in the world, it is impossible to know what this means concretely unless both are willing to sit together and reflect on the "signs of the times" that surround them every day.

The Signs of the Times

A recent Google search on "the signs of the times" turned up an amazing thirty-eight million hits! References cover the spectrum from understanding world events to the Second Coming of Christ. We do not use the term as it is often understood in popular religious discourse, as catastrophic "signs" of the Second Coming of Christ, or of Armageddon.

The term "signs of the times" describes from a faith perspective a method of understanding the current culture in which we live. What Vatican II teaches about the signs of the times must be translated into understanding the culture and the experiences affecting the daily lives of the people in a given community.

Vatican II used "the signs of the times" in *Gaudium et Spes, 4*:

In every age, the Church carries the responsibility of reading the signs of the times and of interpreting them in the light of the Gospel, if it is to carry out its task. In language intelligible to every generation, it should be able to answer the ever recurring questions which people ask about the meaning of this present life and the life to come, and how one is related to the other.

It is essential that the ordained and the laity be able to articulate their understanding of the signs of the times as they live them in their mission field. The dialogue council is geared to a fuller understanding of the meaning of these events as they impact the faith of the people.

~

A pastor interrupted the planned agenda of a pastoral council meeting with a question. He asked how the recent economic downturn in the region was affecting parishioners and the community. There was no mechanism in parish life to determine the effects and how the parish or individual parishioners might respond to those affected.

Without any group preparation, the question, "How are economic conditions affecting our community?" was met with silence. This concern did not exist when the parish's pastoral plan was developed the previous year. This new reality did not fit into the routine agenda of reviewing the parish's success or failure in meeting its goals and objectives. With little to discuss in council, meetings had returned to passively listening to staff progress reports. The unspoken sentiments revolved around the question of why busy people had to be there. What was the urgency of their contribution?

Little by little, after the question was raised, the dialogue in council took a different turn. The community's concerns about the economy now were examined as "signs of the times." These signs required awareness and some action to support parishioners or others caught in job losses or lower wages. The pastor and council entered into several months of reflection on this matter. Gradually, new strategies began to emerge: the parish social ministry team advocated that the parish establish an emergency fund to assist families in transition; food bank personnel were alerted to prepare for additional clients. The pastor was advised to include in his preaching the spiritual implications of living with less in difficult times.

~

If the truth be told, few laity read official Church documents, encyclicals, and pastoral letters. Even if they tried to do so, many would find the language unintelligible and different from their discourse in everyday life. Yet they are expected to live out the principles underlying these teachings in their daily lives and thus be engaged in transforming society.

How are the ordained to assist the laity in understanding and practicing their baptismal mission? How can the laity's life experiences be shared so that the ordained can help them to make these practical applications? Both can be transformed through reflection on the signs of the times.

It takes great sensitivity and compassion to be able to assess and respond to the laity's concerns in living a decent life, raising and supporting a family, and earning a just wage in their work. They need and have the right to pastoral support and spiritual formation to fulfill their baptismal call and mission. With good pastoral care and their own initiative, they can infuse the culture and world with the Gospel values of peace and justice. In addition, the ordained can discover a more fruitful and effective ministry to the laity. The morale of the ordained can also be improved through the transformation that can occur in the dialogue of council.

Council is the unique place where this dialogue can occur. It is a formal structure of the Church. Council is the unique ministry group empowered to identify the signs of the times. The taking of counsel in council precedes pastoral planning and implementation.

Chapter 5

The COUNSEl in council meeting

Gathered at the Table of Council

The table of council is a symbol of gathering and interaction. Some of life's most intimate experiences and conversations occur at the tables in our lives. This image is seen in one pastor's vision of the parish as a table of interaction.

~

After settling into his new pastorate, a priest was asked what he envisioned for the parish. After some pondering, he used the language of "building community." He recalled childhood memories of Sunday and holiday dinners in his Italian grandmother's dining room. "In those days, it was a command performance that all the children and grandchildren were expected to come to Grandma's for Sunday dinner. It seemed that these dinners went on forever. There was always plenty to eat and everyone had a place at the table. Because of those early gatherings, our family has remained in regular contact with each other half a century later.

"My image of the parish," he added, "is a place with many tables where people come together for community, worship, formation, and service. The one to which all are invited, the Sunday dinner table, is the eucharistic table. At the regular Sunday gathering, we experience who we are as a family of faith. The food served is the Word of God and the Body and Blood of Christ. Everyone has a place at this table. At the dismissal, all are sent forth to build up the Body of Christ in the experiences of the coming week.

~

What is the unique purpose of the group who gathers at the "table of council"? How is it different from every other group? Doesn't the pastor consult and interact with many other persons and groups?

Councils, contrary to some current thinking, are not the strategic planners for the faith community. That is not their unique competency or role. They are to engage in the pastoral reflection and the strategic thinking that must precede planning. Planning, decision making, and implementation are necessary steps in a process, but they are not the work of council.

Each time the pastoral council gathers at the table, it is God's time with them, never to be repeated in exactly the same way. "Where two or three are gathered in my name, I am there among them" (Matthew 18:20). It is part of divine providence that this leader and these particular people gather to seek the will of God for this community. It is time graced by the presence of the Holy Spirit.

Each person's "providence" merges and becomes intertwined in this unique gathering. God's will is recognized not only in the deliberations of the council, but also in the relationships that develop among those at the table of council.

The ordained leader must be aware of this special providence and remind the laity consistently that providence will be discovered in the deliberations and in the community that develops among them. It is a shared and corporate journey. Such a community is not a given; it must be created.

Effective council meetings flow from this awareness and require appropriate preparation of the members, active engagement of the members in the meeting, and a distinct time for debriefing afterwards.

The Council Meeting

Preparation for Council

If good counsel is to be given and received, council members must have a sense of what is expected of each of them. What is the subject of the council agenda and what reflection and counsel will be needed?

Wisdom thinking is needed if true counsel is the desired goal. For this to occur, all participants should be prepared for the content of the council meeting. If not, people tend to respond out of their initial feelings or reactions. While some reactions are necessary to understand the minds and hearts of people, this is only the first level. The goal is to move from "feeling" to "wisdom thinking." Preparation forces clearer thinking.

The sources for council agenda are what the pastor is observing in his daily experience in the life of the parish (his mission field), and what the laity are hearing and experiencing in their lives and in the wider community (their mission field).

The following is an example of how an agenda might come about and what preparation members need beforehand.

~

A parish had been in existence for over seventy-five years. Within that time, the neighborhood had changed from white middle class to a large multi-ethnic, racial community. Mass was now celebrated in two or more languages on any given Sunday.

The pastor had been leading this faith community for over ten years and had a growing sense that the seventy-five-year-old church no longer met the needs of this changing community. What to do? On one hand, he realized that the average income of the people was at or below the national average. On the other hand, he recognized that the community was growing and that he had an obligation to provide a future place of worship for the congregation.

His instincts were good: Ask the people, but do so after you have spent time educating them about why this planning for the future is so important. He decided to spend a year in dialogue with the council to hear their experiences and the issues facing households within the changing community. Before each meeting, he forwarded a series of clear questions to the council. He wanted them to have sufficient time to think through the multiple, complex issues.

Each council meeting began with a half hour of prayer and faith sharing. He believed that prayer was an essential part of taking counsel and developed Scripture based faith sharing to focus the deliberations in council. Over the year long process, the pastor discovered many things he did not previously know. This enabled him to think more clearly and objectively about his community and to be better in touch with the real life concerns of the people. New facilities would have to reflect and "facilitate" the pastoral life of this community and not another community.

Two years later, the parish embraced the idea of a new church building and began thinking through a fundraising plan. His willingness to prepare the people to offer good counsel, even with its stresses, was well worth the time and energy. The process of deliberating on a new worship space was as important as the facility itself.

The Meeting: Giving and Receiving Counsel

Council is a formal structure of the Church. It exists to answer one critical question: What is the will of God for this community? This is the ultimate question of a council. All the processes it uses are to answer this question.

As noted above, council meetings are centered in seeking a Gospel response to the signs of the times. These answers cannot be sought outside of a deep commitment to prayer as a group. In another chapter, we will examine the variety of spiritual resources used by a council. It is sufficient here to emphasize that councils are to be rooted in devotion and prayer to the Holy Spirit.

There are several key elements to a council meeting:

~ Every member is expected to speak. Time is given to hear the voices of all the members, not simply the vocal few.
~ Members are invited to share their instincts and feelings as well as their thoughts.
~ After everyone has been heard, individual members' comments can be discussed. To allow discussion prematurely often silences the voices of quieter members. They may hold critical insights that would not be heard.

~ The pastor must ask clarifying questions to assure that he is receiving adequate counsel.

~ The members are invited to moments of silence and reflection on what they have heard from each other.

~ Authentic counsel is given when members can voice their reasons for something as well as their reasons against it. These reasons are then measured against Gospel values.

~ The pastor must take seriously the consensus that has been voiced, especially when a decision is required. Only rarely should a pastor have to make a decision contrary to the counsel he has received.

Councils are human groups. As such, they will develop over time and experience all the dynamics of any other group. Members need to know that their presence is critical and that they are not peripheral to the process. They may have to face conflicts and power struggles between and among them. They need to learn to collaborate with other parish groups and to understand the ultimate decision-making authority of the pastor. The pastor's role should be understood accurately. It should not be over or under emphasized in council.

As a group, ordained and lay members of council may desire to grow in relationship and harmony together. This should be monitored to avoid "group think" or other group dynamics that inhibit the process of giving and taking counsel. A wise pastoral leader attends to these dynamics of the council. If a council desires to become a mature community, it has to be willing to address its conflicts.

After the Meeting: Debriefing

It is not uncommon that participants gather informally "in the parking lot" to express their feelings after a meeting. Some of this venting may uncover important insights about council that should not be lost. Therefore, we propose that the "parking lot meeting" be incorporated into the meeting agenda.

All council meetings should include a time for everyone to reflect on the outcomes and results of the meeting. The purpose for doing this is for all to look at their corporate behavior and to find ways to improve future council meetings.

The post meetings can be called the *blunder council.*[2] Members are asked to examine their personal conduct during the meeting, as well as the working of the group as a whole. Was the group respectful? Did it listen well? Did everyone get an opportunity to speak? Did someone dominate? If so, why was such behavior tolerated? What helped to take and give counsel? What prevented this from happening?

Members can be asked to identify what would make the next meeting even better. Over time, these post sessions move quickly as members become more conscious of their own and the group's behavior.

Confidentiality is an essential element of all council deliberations. Does the council operate under articulated rules of confidentiality? Is the council faithful to these rules? What breaches of confidentiality may result in removal from council? Is this understood by all members of council? Any conflicts that emerge should be processed in the blunder council.

~

Due to enrollment and financial issues, a parish was faced with the decision to either close the school or merge with a nearby school. The parish was equally divided; the most vocal school supporters sought to keep the school open at all costs. Others, less interested and less vocal, saw the inevitable need to close.

The pastor sought counsel in council and asked for the utmost candor from council members in deliberating the school's future. The discussions were heated; the council could not reach unanimity on a recommendation to the pastor and deliberations were postponed to the next month. Shortly thereafter, individual council members and the pastor began receiving angry and threatening emails from irate stakeholders in the school. Obviously, word had leaked about those in council who favored and those who opposed a recommendation for closure/merger.

At the next meeting, the pastor confronted the council with the facts and asked who was responsible for divulging very sensitive information that had been shared in confidence. Many admitted that they had no idea that the conversations in council were confidential. It had never been discussed. Eventually, however, the culprits identified themselves and defended their reasons.

The pastor then took counsel from the group about how to handle the matter. His question was: Should he ask for the resignations of those who spoke out of turn, and/or should the council revisit the sacred role and privileged forum of council?

Since confidentiality had not been universally understood, it was necessary to renegotiate the rules binding all members before moving forward.

~

The moral of the story: Council is serious business.

Chapter 6

Spiritual Practices Used in Council

The dialogue in council is geared to helping the pastor make prudent decisions by avoiding simplistic judgments, jumping to premature conclusions, or looking for generic answers in canned solutions or programs.

Prayer, reflection, dialogue, and wisdom thinking are required before any planning might or might not take place. There is no other forum in parish life where this quality of reflective dialogue can occur.

The disciplined use of spiritual practices is required to engage in reflective conversations about the pastoral mission. Several methods can be used. Since these spiritual practices are not commonly known or used by many, catechesis and formation of council is needed. Spiritual development as a group must also be fostered.

Four distinct spiritual activities can be used appropriately in council. They are faith sharing, mission (apostolic or pastoral), reflection, theological reflection, and discernment.

Faith Sharing

We read in Matthew 18:20: "Where two or three are gathered in my name, I am there among them." Jesus offers no limits, rules, or outlines; it was just that simple. However, his presence must be invoked and then welcomed. The means for achieving this have been developed and are found formally in the spiritual traditions of the Church. Faith sharing is one of these traditions.

Faith sharing is a group activity in which individuals are given the opportunity to reflect together upon a passage of sacred Scripture. The purpose is for individual spiritual growth and for the spiritual growth of the group as a whole.

Each person is encouraged to seek insight into his or her life considering the Scripture passage and to develop the capacity to share this with others as a member of the council.

Faith sharing is most often used as a form of prayer at the beginning of council meetings. Faith sharing is the foundation for other group processes such as mission reflection and discernment.

Faith sharing includes several steps:

~ Selection of an appropriate Scripture passage, and reading the passage aloud in the group and/or quietly as an individual.
~ Time for quiet reflection on the meaning or message of the passage as it applies to one's own life. The following questions apply:
  • What is happening in my life, in me?
  • What is happening in this passage of Scripture?
  • How does it relate to my life and experience?
  • What insight(s), encouragement, or challenge do I receive in reflecting on this passage?
  • What do I feel drawn to share with others or the group?

~ At the leader's request, members share these insights either with another person or with the entire group.

~ When individuals begin to speak, others are asked to listen without comment.

~ When everyone is finished, members of the council are invited to reflect on what they have heard from each other.

~ Faith sharing can close with a rereading of the Scripture passage, with a group reflection on the insights given, or with a closing prayer. Members can be invited to offer their insights about the presence of the wisdom in the group sharing.

Through their reflective listening, the council members open themselves to receive the gift of wisdom and become more receptive to what the Holy Spirit is revealing in the group. Faith sharing is never an end in itself. It is a means to alert members to the working of the Holy Spirit in summoning them to mission.

At a certain point in the council meeting, the pastor or leader may ask the members to return to the Scripture and the insights that have been shared. If necessary, members may be asked to respond again to what they have heard in the discussion. This is very important if there is an issue or a conflict blocking creative thinking or discussion. It is also important when fuller discussion is deemed necessary.

~

The Council meeting began with the Gospel reading, Mark 4:35–41 (Jesus calms the storm at sea). Everyone shared an insight about the passage, and each individual could easily identify with Jesus being tired and with the panic of the disciples. The council meeting continued.

The agenda that followed focused on how the parish

should help provide formation for parishioners in preparation for voting in an election year. The council immediately felt the tensions among themselves as the discussion ensued. One woman pointed out that their discussion was getting into a stormy sea! She suggested that they stop and reread the passage. Her suggestion was received with mixed and mostly negative reactions. The pastor agreed and everyone went back to the passage to discover if the Word of God had any direct relevance to the "storm" brewing in the parish and in the council at this moment.

Members were more subdued this time. Their reflection this time centered on the struggle of the disciples, upset that Jesus appeared to be sleeping (not with them) in the storm. "After all," said one of the men, "it isn't as though they were neophytes at sea!"

When the pastor invited them back to the agenda, one man remarked that he was beginning to better understand the "stormy" issue on the table. Others agreed, and the meeting continued with members' greater appreciation of the counsel that the pastor was seeking from the council.

~

When a group is blocked or emotions are running high, facilitators often recommend that the group "take five" and give the participants some time to regain perspective. This is not enough for a faith community. Unless the council is intractable, the proper practice of faith sharing can help the members to develop greater insight by facing the issues at hand instead of avoiding them. This will take time and practice. As faith sharing becomes a regular practice in council, members themselves become more comfortable with it and are more prone to return to it as needed.

Mission Reflection

Mission reflection is the process used to seek deeper understanding of current events in light of the Gospel and the values of the culture. It can be used by an individual or a group. It is also referred to as apostolic or pastoral reflection. It is an important process used in coming to a deeper understanding of "inculturation."

Culture is a set of shared values, practices, symbols, rituals, and goals that hold together any group or nation. Culture is also used to describe the unique ways peoples live in different parts of the world and in a local community. This usually includes the way they dress, the food they eat, their language and customs. For example, we speak about "American" culture as different from "French" culture. Within American culture we can also speak of the culture of California as different from that of Rhode Island.

Culture brings a sense of order to our lives, a sense of belonging. Often we do not appreciate our sense of order in our own culture until we visit another country or place. Families have their own "culture." When couples marry, they will often speak about their in-laws as though they were foreigners (even if they reside down the block). In a marriage, two family cultures intersect "for better or for worse."

We live and work within a culture that is a composite of various other cultures. No matter what the culture may be, it is the place to which we are to bring God's love. The process of doing this is referred to as "inculturation."

Mission reflection is an integral part of inculturation. Mission reflection enables us to identify those things in our daily lives which "shock" our faith. It helps us to identify the gap that exists between the Gospel teachings and the present reality.

Mission reflection has a specific focus: the mission as it is being lived out in everyday life within one's culture. It is a way of looking at what we do through the lens of the Gospel. It is a way of examining our culture through this same lens. Mission reflection also invites us to go deeper into understanding culture and the Gospel.

Mission reflection begins in a dialogue about:

~ What is happening in our daily work, daily providence, daily experiences of living. *"The apostles gathered around Jesus, and told him all that they had done and taught"* (Mark 6:30).
~ The cultural reality in which we are living this daily reality. *"For many were coming and going, and they had no leisure even to eat"* (Mark 6:31).
~ The message of the Gospel in relationship to these two. *"As he went ashore, he saw a great crowd; and he had compassion for them, because they were like sheep without a shepherd; and he began to teach them many things"* (Mark 6:34).

Mission reflection then asks three critical questions:

~ What are the positive and negative values of the culture in which we work or minister?
~ What are our personal or communal values?
~ How are these in harmony – or not – with the Gospel?

These critical questions always lead to the last and most important one: "What are we to do to accomplish our stated mission?"

Mission response is determined by understanding the gap that exists between the culture and the Gospel. Mission reflection helps us to separate out a social service response from a faith-based response offered to those in need. It recognizes that all

human need has a spiritual dimension. Too often, either the human or the spiritual dimensions are viewed exclusively to the detriment of both. For example, mission reflection can help us to understand the difference between a healing (the spiritual experience of inclusion) and a concrete cure (a visible physical improvement).

Faith sharing and mission reflection are important tools that should be integrated into council work. Members should be taught, encouraged, and monitored in their growth in each distinct practice.

~

Don, a member of the council, noticed that greater numbers of people were seeking food at the community food bank. He was disturbed by this knowledge (faith shock) and went to the team who ran it. He wanted to know what he and his family could do. He gave them a generous check, but also said that he would visit one family to better assess the problem. He wanted to understand the gap between the reality and the Gospel teachings.

That Tuesday, he went to the Council meeting. He had no intention of placing this on the council agenda, because he did not think that this was a concern of the pastor or the council. During the prayer and faith sharing, Don spoke about visiting a family who was a client of the food bank. He expressed great sadness that people in the community lived this way. Something happened. The council got quiet. When the faith sharing was completed, a council member asked if they could hear more from Don. All agreed. The pastor sat quietly as Don told the story and raised the questions. What are we to do?

What followed was a remarkable council meeting. Each council member began to reflect on the circumstances of the local community in which they all lived. The pastor led them back into Scripture reflection as it reflected on the community reality. He later related that this was one of the best council meetings he had ever witnessed. He said, "It was the first time I really understood mission reflection. Everyone began to ponder what God was asking of them and of the community. And it came from the everyday life of the laity!"

~

Jesus used parables as a form of mission reflection. These parables always spoke to a reality, often right in front of the listener. He described the injustices and the struggles of all peoples. As he told the story, Jesus involved and challenged the community to respond. The community included the disciples and all those who heard his voice. Some responded and others turned away. To those who heard his voice and followed him, he promised an eternal relationship with God.

Questions for Mission Reflection

1. If Jesus was visibly present in our community or parish today, what issues or concerns would be in his parables?
2. Who are the abandoned people or causes? Where do we meet them in this community?
3. In what way are these abandoned people or situations in need of our pastoral response and care?

Theological Reflection

Theological reflection illuminates our understanding of a situation or experience and helps answer the question, "How is this situation or experience related to the teachings of our Catholic faith?"

In her book, *Fostering Leadership Skills in Ministry,* Jean Marie Hiesberger expresses the idea this way:

The basic premise of such theological reflection is that there is truly an intimate relationship between our lives and our religious heritage, our beliefs. Theological reflection is the process that helps us discover that relationship, to see what one of them says to the other. To the extent that we see and try to live out that connection, to make our faith relevant and vibrant in all parts of our lives, we are able to live an authentic Christian life.[3]

Pastoral councils engage in theological reflection as a group, especially as they become more aware of what the Church teaches and what they are being asked to do. Theological reflection taps into the wisdom of the ages. For example: How does Scripture challenge our materialism? What is the Church's social teaching on immigration, life issues, poverty, racism? What is the teaching of the Church on the Eucharist and the building of the community? On the sacraments? On the holiness of the laity in everyday life?

Theological reflection is the dynamic interplay among (a) our religious tradition; (b) the culture in which we live; and (c) our unique experience as a community. It is the foundation for mission reflection as it helps us to shape pastoral responses based on the long traditions of the Church.

~

Don's and the parish's response to the growing poverty of the
community is based in a deep tradition of the Church, which
is based in Scripture and Catholic social teaching. Church
teaching provides the foundation and the structure that move
us to respond as the baptized.

In this particular situation, the pastor invited the members of the council to a guided reflection on Pope Benedict's
encyclical, *Caritas in Veritate*. He pointed out the rich heritage of teaching on the social mission of the Church. He also
reflected with them that this mission is primarily carried out
in everyday life by the laity. Don's concern about the changing
reality around him was indeed the mission of the Church in
the world—in his world.

Discernment

Do not be conformed to this world,
but be transformed by the renewing of your minds,
so that you may discern what is the will of God—
what is good and acceptable and perfect.

ROMANS: 12:2

Discernment is the intentional practice by which an individual
or community seeks, recognizes, and chooses to take part in the
activity of God in concrete situations. The aim of discernment is
to enhance one's participation in the work of God, to promote the
glory of God and to share in God's desire for the healing and transformation of the world. There is no single method that guarantees
how the Holy Spirit will be discerned because it cannot be captured
in any formula.

Discernment is about God's work done in and through us. It is about our thoughts, feelings, and actions and their potential to reveal the reign of God in the moment. It is about how we choose to use our talents, time, and resources for the glory of God. Discernment touches into the mystery of God's plan for us by faithfully reflecting on where we are being drawn—negatively and positively. It is grounded in humble self-knowledge. It is based in an honest relationship with God in Christ and in a desire to be God's instrument for the healing of the world.

Communal discernment presupposes that individuals have had some personal experience of discernment. Father William Barry writes:

> Communal discernment presupposes before all else that those who will engage in it have experienced the discernment of spirits in themselves....Communal discernment presupposes that the individuals can and will communicate their experiences in prayer and in prayerful reflection to others....But the willingness to communicate experience must also be present, and this is often the rock upon which attempts at communal discernment shatter.[4]

Effective group or communal discernment requires a limited number of people. It involves time and commitment to a process. Pastoral councils may engage in corporate discernment when they find themselves at certain crossroads and must seek the greater good for the community. In such a case, discernment also considers the thoughts, feelings, resources, and gifts of the community. Discernment always seeks the greater good, even if suffering may ensue.

We do not offer here any specific process for discernment. It is a process used when a greater good is sought. It brings to light all those things that might stand in the way of coming to a right and just decision.

Discernment is not to be used to make the final decision. It is a way of identifying all those things that will enlighten the person responsible for the decision. Ultimately, in council, it is the pastor who must make the final decision and who is responsible for its implementation. Discernment always calls for fortitude.

~

A mosque was being built within a changing neighborhood in a large city. Once the stronghold of Irish immigrants, the area had changed over the years. The people who lived in the neighborhood were now of mixed faith traditions, and many resented the influx of Muslims into the community.

Some of the Catholics went to the pastor and demanded a "review" of the situation. They wanted to know what he was going to do about it! In his wisdom, he invited ten community leaders to a "discernment" evening. In the first session, he invited this group to engage in four weeks of personal and public prayer together at certain times. He presented them with a format to use. The questions asked them to reflect upon what God wanted in this situation. What did each person think God wanted him to do? What had they already done? Where and how did they seek God's guidance? Might they be using "God's will" as a cover for their own agendas? They were to name their fears, concerns, and what they thought might be blessings. At the end of the four weeks, the ten were invited to a day of reflection together. Most of the time was spent in respectful listening to each other's insights and feelings.

The people wanted the pastor to "do something." He wisely

realized that he first needed reflection and serious, thoughtful conversation. The people lived in the community and interacted on a daily basis with people of all faiths and cultures. He believed that the role of the parish was to prepare them for this reality through a constant "discernment" of God's will in any given time. His decision was to continue to invite the parishioners to a deeper time of prayer and understanding of their changing situation. He believed the Holy Spirit would show the community the right answer. Meanwhile, they were encouraged to pray and offer hospitality to one another. Today this parish continues to work at accepting and understanding their Muslim neighbors.

Addendum on Consensus

The word "consensus" in daily use is equated with a group's collective agreement, a collaborative process rather than a compromise. Genuine consensus typically requires focus on a group's relationships as its members seek to make a decision. The locus of authority is within the group.

In Canon Law, the locus of ecclesial authority is given by appointment to canonical offices. In a diocese, the diocesan bishop is the legitimate authority. He delegates authority to the pastor of a parish.

Pastoral councils can utilize the consensus process effectively as long as it is understood that the locus of authority for the final decision resides within the pastor, not within the council itself. The hierarchical structure of the Church cannot be circumvented. A council gives counsel, proposes, or recommends. The ordained leader takes or receives counsel and then exercises his authority when he decides and acts. Such is the canonical structure of the Church.

There are those who criticize the Church and the "ultimate

authority" of the ordained. Some of this anger may be justified, as negative experiences from the past conflicts abound. Some criticism is unreasonable and polarizing. Some of it may also reflect dissent or discontent with other areas of ecclesial life.

No human being is omni-competent. All organizations, including the family, have hierarchy. All organizations have someone who is responsible to make ultimate decisions. Even when a consensus process is followed, someone ultimately takes the responsibility to carry forward or discount the will of the group. Good leadership consists of knowing when and how to evoke authority.

It must also be said that the laity encounter "hierarchy" in their workplace and all strata of society. Hierarchy is especially visible in the workplace when employees brainstorm, ask questions, work in subcommittees, or chair committees—all for the purpose of making recommendations on a product or service. Ultimately, the decision to implement such recommendations resides in the authority of someone else, usually corporate leaders. All this is part of American life, even in a democracy.

Consensus is effective only to the degree that the group keeps its focus on the long term implications of its actions. Consensus works best when it unleashes the group's creativity abilities rather than its need for power. If power and control issues exist, they are best addressed directly and forthrightly.

True "power" in ecclesial life, including at the table of council, will always be exercised in the capacity for open and mature dialogue between ordained and laity about the concrete signs of the times affecting the Church's pastoral mission in a given place and time.

Chapter 7

Virtues and Gifts in Council: Rooted in Baptism

The Grace and Call of Baptism

The gifts of the Holy Spirit given in baptism impel us to live the Christian life of discipleship. This discipleship is expressed in conscious and active participation in the Church's liturgical and sacramental life. The baptized are to lead lives of prayer, and they are called to participate in family and community, in the search for justice, and to love in all circumstances of life—especially the least of God's children, the poor and abandoned. They are called to do this not periodically in extraordinary circumstances, but within the providence of their everyday lives.

With the grace of baptism also comes the call of baptism. Grace empowers call. The sacramental initiation into this life and call in baptism is completed in confirmation and Eucharist. Christian living is a graced participation in the life of the Trinity. It is made concrete in the search for personal holiness and is expressed in the habitual practice of virtue.

Christians are not baptized only for themselves or merely for their individual or personal salvation. There is more to baptism than the removal of original sin. The call and mission of the baptized is to participate in the transformation of the world. Baptism is linked to the sending of the Church into the whole world in Matthew 28:19. It makes the baptized witnesses to Christ in the world and is the foundation for the priesthood of all believers who are sent to proclaim the mighty acts of God (1 Peter 2:5, 9). Baptism is the sacrament of initiation and of mission for all.

Life in the Holy Spirit

The theological virtues of faith, hope and charity—and the gifts of the Holy Spirit—are received in baptism. The Holy Spirit empowers us to use these gifts and virtues in fulfillment of the baptismal mission.

Councils also need the guidance of the Holy Spirit to learn the will of God for the community. They need the strength of the Spirit to move forward in fortitude. A council cannot act in a virtuous manner without seeking the assistance and guidance of the Holy Spirit.

The answer to the question, "How are we to do this?" will not be found on a list of "best practices" of the latest successful organizations. The answer to this "how" question—a pearl of great price—is in the midst of the Church herself.

The Cardinal Virtues Applicable in Council

Prudence and Fortitude

One of *Aesop's Fables* is the story of the thirsty crow that sees a pitcher with water. Alas, the water is too low in the bottom of the pitcher for the crow to reach. What to do? The crow is very thirsty, so he wisely sets out to raise the water level. He begins by picking up a pebble into his beak and placing it into the pitcher. Back and forth! Pebble after pebble! Little by little! Eventually the water rises high enough and the wise crow is able to quench his thirst!

This story has implications for this chapter on the virtues operative in council. This book is based on the assumption that divine wisdom, the gift of the Holy Spirit, can be more fully recognized in the dialogue that takes place in council between the ordained and the laity. They seek to interpret the signs of the times in which they exist.

Wisdom is not given completely to an individual or group alone. It is visible and operative in the dynamic between and among them. Back and forth, little by little, pebble by pebble, true counsel is achieved through the consistent and faithful attempt to bridge their fields of mission. Counsel is attained ultimately only through a disciplined use of specific gifts and virtues.

Virtues are attitudes, dispositions, or character traits that enable us to be and act in ways that develop our full potential personally and within a group or community. Christian virtue is the response to the calling to "put on the new self, created in God's way in righteousness and holiness of truth" (Ephesians 4:24).

The habits of virtue are acquired through learning and continual practice. A developed virtue becomes a defined way of living and governs our actions with other people. Virtues, once acquired, become characteristic of a person, group, or community. They are never developed in isolation from the community or from our interactions with others.

Books have been written and workshops given on being a virtuous leader in the last few decades. Most of the literature applies the practice of certain virtues to a company's financial success. Here we look at virtue and the gifts of baptism as the means to live more fully the life in God in us. Critical to the process of council are the gifts of the Holy Spirit—*wisdom* and *counsel*—and the cardinal virtues of *prudence* and *fortitude*. We examine these gifts and virtues and their practical application to council.

Prudence

> *Precaution is better than cure.*
>
> CICERO

Prudence is wisdom in handling practical matters. It is exercising good judgment or common sense. It disposes us in all circumstances to form right judgments about what we must do or not do. It is the most important of the cardinal or moral virtues, for it directs the other virtues in choosing the proper means in obtaining their respective goals. Without this virtue, one will not choose well, nor live a life corresponding to the final goal of life. It is not enough to want to do good; one must choose the means to achieve the good. The practice of prudence can keep individuals or groups from falling into the pitfalls that lead to poor decision-making.

Fortitude

> *I believe that I shall see the goodness of the Lord*
> *   in the land of the living.*
> *Wait for the Lord;*

be strong, and let your heart take courage;
wait for the Lord!

PSALM 27:13–14

Fortitude, a cardinal virtue and a gift of the Holy Spirit, is the strength of mind that allows persons to endure necessary pain or adversity with courage. It is courage, the firmness in facing difficulties and constancy in the pursuit of the good. Fortitude strengthens the resolve to resist temptations and to overcome obstacles in the moral life. It ultimately disposes persons to be able to sacrifice their lives if necessary.

If prudence is the virtue of seeing the correct decision to be made, fortitude is the courage and patience to endure whatever obstacles that might interfere with the process of decision making or implementation of decisions.

The Gifts of the Holy Spirit in Council

Of the Gifts of the Holy Spirit (Isaiah 11:2–3), two particular gifts are operative in the process of council: Wisdom and Counsel.

Wisdom

My child, if you accept my words
    and treasure up my commandments within you,
making your ear attentive to wisdom
    and inclining your heart to understanding;
if you indeed cry out for insight,
    and raise your voice for understanding;
if you seek it like silver,
    and search for it as for hidden treasures—
then you will understand the fear of the Lord

and find the knowledge of God.
For the Lord gives wisdom;
*   from his mouth come knowledge and understanding;*

PROVERBS 2:1–6

Human wisdom is a composite of common sense and good judgment. It is learning and erudition. It suggests great understanding of people, of situations, and good judgment in dealing with them. Wisdom enables one to focus on the unseen consequences in determining the next steps to take; it provides simple, practical solutions in the midst of conflict and confusion. Wisdom is practical knowledge rooted in experience; wise actions flow from this knowledge.

In the realm of the spiritual, the gift of wisdom is the capacity the Lord gives to know what insights may best be applied to specific needs arising at specific times in our lives. It is a deep insight and understanding of the things of God as reflected in Solomon's prayer:

Send her [wisdom] forth from your holy heavens
and from your glorious throne dispatch her
that she may be with me and work with me,
that I may know what is your pleasure.

WISDOM 9:10

Wisdom is the practical ability to apply the truths discovered, to make practical and skillful application of these to life's situations. Wisdom focuses on the unseen circumstances in determining the next steps to take. It provides simple, practical solutions in the midst of conflict and confusion. In its most profound form, wisdom gives the individual and the community the special ability to judge human things according to God's standards. As such, it has a special place in the process of council.

Counsel

In human affairs, counsel is the assistance given to an individual or group to assist in achieving greater clarity, freedom, and motivation to be able to live a more balanced life. As a gift of the Holy Spirit, counsel is referred to as "right judgment." It renders the person docile and open to God's wisdom and disposed to receive the inspiration of the Holy Spirit. It provides a solution to many difficult and unexpected situations and problems.

Counsel enlightens the person from within about what to do, especially in important matters. The gift of counsel perfects prudence. It enlightens the moral choices presented in daily life. Through the practice of counsel, one penetrates the true meaning of Gospel values especially as expressed in the Beatitudes.

Father Shaun McCarty, ST, distinguishes the gift of counsel from spiritual discernment.

> *Counsel is a gift that helps keep one soft hearted (not hard hearted) as well as hard headed (not soft headed). It makes a person docile to the living God. Docility is necessary to hear, to perceive, to learn. It means literally to be "teachable." God enlightens persons so they can make decisions to do specific things in accord with the divine will, which decisions extend God's (kingdom) reign.* [5]

Counsel is the Spirit-guided ability to enter into the experience of others to heal and to enable growth. Counsel is needed especially when it is difficult to understand God's love and providence in a situation. Counsel helps one to know when to accept something as God's providence or to fight against it because it is not.

The gift of counsel raises the virtue of prudence to a new dimension. It not only suggests what to do in the long range, but also what to do in the practical details of our daily lives. The more open we are to the Spirit, the more the Spirit takes over our lives. The inspirations of counsel are closer to us than spoken directives. Through these inspirations, God is intimately present to us and is always available and accessible if we are open to it.

Do councils need virtuous people? This question can be answered with another: Does the Christian life demand the practice of virtue? The answer to both is "yes." A true council emerges as it develops the capacity to operate out of virtuous choices. Virtuous choices demand a disciplined way of being, thinking, and acting in concert.

Councils do not become virtuous without hard and intentional work. If individual virtue is acquired through repetitious good action, then the same holds true for a group or community. A "corporate will" can only be developed through a conscious choice by council members to choose to use prudence and wisdom as the basis for good counsel and to choose fortitude when action is needed. As the laity and the ordained grow in these practical virtues, council becomes more refined in the ability to recommend appropriate pastoral responses.

The Virtues and Gifts in Council

Prudence in Council

Prudence shapes the manner in which pastoral leaders make good decisions. It is therefore a foundational element in the process of seeking counsel. The prudent person works hard to come to a clearer and more accurate understanding of the "big picture" of any situation in order to make the best possible decision(s) on how to address it. Prudence will dictate what is to be done or avoided. The virtue of fortitude flows from prudence.

A new pastor, for example, would be well advised to seek counsel from a pastoral council on major issues such as how best to understand the parish's history, parishioners' current concerns, the way the parishioners handle change, their feelings about the past, economic and social issues in the community, etc. A prudent assessment of such matters is a prerequisite for authorizing any pastoral plan of action. The practice of prudence will challenge and bring to light a new pastor's overt or covert biases. It is prudent for him to carefully assess to appreciate the legitimate influence and accomplishments of his predecessor(s). Prudence will also challenge the inevitable temptations to clerical sibling rivalry (for example, feeling the need to "undo" his predecessor's decisions or projects) and to impose his will prematurely on a new community of people.

Council is the privileged and appropriate forum in which to have such important deliberations. Imprudent or precipitous decisions will only inhibit ministry. The ultimate concern is not what the leader or group thinks should happen, but how the Holy Spirit is moving in this period of transition in the parish and community.

~

The new pastor, within weeks of his arrival, wanted to renovate the sanctuary of the church to his liturgical tastes. He was surprised at a council meeting when one member, Marie, asked him about rumors she had heard in the parish about his intentions. When he outlined his ideas, the council members became silent until someone challenged the project—or at least his timing.

They agreed that since he was not yet well-known to the parishioners, time and attention should be directed to other pressing priorities of the people. In addition, the parish was running a small deficit in its operating budget with no funds available for such a project. In the dialogue that ensued, the pastor was able to hear the points raised and decided that while his project had merit, it was not an objective priority and lacked a compelling rationale. The truth that emerged: It would be premature and imprudent to embark on a capital project so early into his pastorate. Having taken this wise counsel, he decided to set aside his personal preferences and began engaging the council about the deeper concerns facing parishioners.

~

When pastoral councils remain silent or simply "rubber stamp" a pastor's ideas or behavior, they are not practicing the virtues of wisdom, prudence, or counsel. They have abdicated their representation of their mission field and the virtue of fortitude. Virtue is only attained in a council the more it is chosen and used.

Fortitude in Council

Pastoral leaders face conflicts and challenges in coming to important decisions. As alluded to earlier, they can be immobilized in making decisions by internal obstacles (for example, anxieties about making decisions) or external obstacles (for example, fear of the reactions of those affected by decisions). If pastoral leaders are committed to the discernment of God's will over their own, regardless of its cost, the virtue of fortitude will assist them in remaining undaunted in implementing decisions that affect the good of the wider community over the interests of the few or even their own.

~

A pastor and council were in dialogue about the implications of the parish's dwindling number of members and deteriorating finances. The future was bleak and the inevitability of closure or merger was becoming obvious. They could not make the pastoral recommendation on the issue before them. It became clear that both the leader and council were experiencing deep resistance and fear. The resistance was not based on a lack of understanding of the facts, but in a lack of will to do what they knew had to be done. They lacked the courage to act.

~

After the pastor has taken counsel and has reached a decision, the virtue of fortitude is required for implementation. Fortitude is operative for the council members also as they commit to supporting and promoting the decision, regardless of conflicts that may ensue.

Wisdom in Council

A council does not attain wisdom automatically or without great effort. That effort requires such things in council as the openness to accept differing opinions and the capacity to think independently, awareness of what is happening in the community in which they live and work, and a willingness and capacity to surrender private or personal opinions for the good of the whole. Wisdom is also attained when council members can move through undifferentiated feeling to clear thinking in deliberations. Pastoral council members must ultimately believe that each person holds a piece of the truth and that there is a larger, corporate wisdom in the council as a whole than in individual members.

~

Each year a small rural parish in the Midwest welcomed seasonal workers who helped local farmers harvest their crops. The parish had welcomed and integrated them into the faith community.

One summer, a young parishioner was killed in an automobile accident with a worker who was driving drunk with his friends. This completely devastated her family, the parish, and the community. Rage broke out immediately in the community; the desire for vengeance was palpable.

The pastor of the now divided parish convened the council immediately. Over the years, he had helped to form them into a structure where truth could be spoken and wise decisions could be reached. However, this was a new challenge. When he asked for counsel on how to address the situation, there was great hesitancy at first. He pushed for prudence and wisdom in the dialogue so that a right judgment could be made and vengeance rejected. Little by little, different people spoke up about the issues of the seasonal workers, issues that had existed for years but were never addressed.

The council members spoke openly and honestly. One member employed seasonal workers and felt directly implicated. There was great ambivalence in the group as they pondered how the parish community would bury the girl and what would be the place of the driver.

After much dialogue and prayer to the Holy Spirit, the pastor came to a decision. Each member prayed for the pastor as he took the responsibility to address the complexities of the situation.

On the day of the funeral, the dead girl's brother came into the church holding the arm of the driver. They both stood near the coffin facing the people. In a halting voice, the driver of the car asked for forgiveness from the family. The brother, acting in the name of the girl's family, asked him to join them in the pew. They had spoken with the police and had requested that, for the time of funeral liturgy, the driver be allowed to be "forgiven" and be seated with the family.

~

When relating this story, the pastor emphasized that the council had operated with great virtue. He believed that this helped to avert serious community issues and that the injustices of the migrant workers' lives would change. He also stated that perhaps over these years, he himself had been too focused on parish programs and not enough on hearing the deeper issues that affected parish and community life. He felt that, henceforth, these were the kinds of concerns that needed to be brought to council meetings.

Wisdom is the capacity to focus on the unseen circumstances in determining the next steps to take. It can help provide simple practical solutions in the midst of turmoil and conflict. This was certainly the case in the above story. The pastor truly believed that God's wisdom would emerge in the deliberations of the council. The outcome would be a decision based on God's plan and not pandering to human passions.

Counsel in Council

In the above story, the pastor sought counsel on a very serious pastoral issue in the community. He recognized that the parishioners were the ones living in the middle of the concerns. He encouraged them to see God's presence and love in this terrible situation and to grapple with what, in faith, they had to do. In that case, by giving

and taking counsel, the council was able to grow and eventually
work toward greater healing in the community.

Counsel can only be given when the other virtues are at work in
the group. Counsel is not the same as consultation. Counsel probes
the circumstances and differentiates between the acceptance of what
is God's providence and what should be rejected.

By the practice of giving counsel, members entered into the felt
experience of all the involved parties. It was not easy to offer counsel about the drunk driver. However, they persevered and sought
to understand God's abiding love for him, for the young girl, and
for her family. By practicing virtues and employing the gifts of the
Holy Spirit, the council encouraged the pastor to go forward with
fortitude in the face of great anger and hurt.

> *A shoot shall come out from the stock of Jesse,*
> *and a branch shall grow out of his roots.*
> *The spirit of the Lord shall rest on him,*
> *the spirit of wisdom and understanding,*
> *the spirit of counsel and might,*
> *the spirit of knowledge and the fear of the Lord.*
> *His delight shall be in the fear of the Lord.*
>
> ISAIAH 11:1–3

Chapter 8

FORMATION FOR COUNCIL: Ordained and Laity

Laity

Today there is great concern in forming the laity for ministry. Lay formation programs and workshops abound. As the mission-driven vision of council develops, what kind of formation is required of council members?

The laity are formed primarily in the crucible of their everyday life experiences. This is too often overlooked. The laity have acquired professional skills through education and in the jobs they hold. Most are successful in their jobs and professions and look upon their family with great pride. Some are top executives, founders of companies, and community leaders. Who hasn't met mothers who multi-task daily: transporting children, preparing meals, and attending to numerous commitments and concerns? Many of them also hold jobs or are single parents. This is a significant influence in their formation.

Their formation continues in other personal arenas as well. For many, work and family life create financial and emotional stress. They must endure worry and suffering, whether poor, middle class, or affluent. They seek meaning in their lives, especially the meaning that comes from their faith. Their field of mission is rarely a straight path. It can be filled with land mines.

Their formation is less academic and theological, but it is real and it is the locus of the Holy Spirit's presence in their lives. Any additional formation should focus primarily on helping them develop the practical skills of articulating and interpreting the deeper meaning of their daily life experiences.

Ordained

Priestly formation occurs in a seminary environment with some degree of pastoral contact with the laity. The focus of their academic, pastoral, and spiritual formation is on the future role they will assume in the Church.

Seminarians must learn through experience how to translate their theological training into sound pastoral practice. This is their lifelong task. To this end, their continuing formation cannot occur without developing sound and appropriate pastoral relationships with the laity. Due to the rapidity of cultural change, relevant pastoral leadership and ministry will require regular and lifelong learning.

Most dioceses provide various tracts of continuing formation for clergy. Some priests are sent for specialized studies in service to the Church. Today, many candidates come to the seminary seeking ordination as a second career and consequently bring with them many professional competencies.

What is said above about the joys and sorrows of the laity also applies to the ordained. They must learn through the crucible of experience how to "connect the dots" between faith and life for themselves and in the lives of the people they serve. Their field of mission, too, is rarely a straight path and is also filled with land mines.

Challenges to Both

If these two mission fields are to come together in fruitful dialogue at the table of council, the formation of both the laity and the ordained will need to incorporate these important elements:

1. Laity must learn a new language and a new style of meeting. They also have to deal with their own cognitive dissonance in relating to the ordained in a mature way. While they have no problem speaking confidently in secular matters, they must learn the art of expressing themselves appropriately to their pastors without fear or deference.
2. The ordained must be able to respect the life and experience of the laity as equally important as – and complementary to – their own. This implies learning how to listen and understand their issues and concerns, and how best to translate these into identifiable pastoral responses in the parish.
3. Both the laity and the ordained must learn how to speak and take counsel from each other. This implies the capacity to respect the uniqueness of each other's wisdom.
4. Laity must learn how to be engaged in conversations of a pastoral nature and to appreciate the unique perspective and pastoral concerns of the ordained.
5. The ordained must learn to listen to the laity's voice so that they can more fully grasp the serious pastoral challenges the laity face in their daily existence.
6. Ordained and laity alike must learn the reflective skills for examining the "signs of the times." This is a challenge in the

hyperactive and non-reflective culture of today's world for both. While the laity may practice their Catholic faith regularly, they probably spend more time with TV, cell phones, computers, and other media than with sacred Scripture or in prayer. Their spirituality may be consciously lived only on the periphery of their daily concerns. Even though the ordained follow a prescribed prayer life, their reflection on their daily life experience may not be as routine as their regular presiding at the Eucharistic liturgy.

The questions of council will always center on what God is asking of us. What are we seeing, hearing, feeling, thinking? What does the wisdom embodied in the tradition of the Church say to these concerns? Ultimately, how are we as a Church to respond?

The United States Catholic Bishops, in their 1986 pastoral letter, "Economic Justice for All," restate the truth that holiness is not confined to the world of private spirituality but is achieved in the midst of the world.

Formation Within the Council Meeting

As emphasized earlier, the taking of counsel is dependent upon the laity and ordained reflecting together on the signs of the times and exploring their meaning in light of each other's field of mission. We highlighted the importance of spiritual methodologies that are integral to taking counsel. Specific virtues were also explored as these help to create the correct environment for each council gathering.

To take counsel in council also entails that the members keep abreast of recent Church teachings as well as all other materials that are helpful to their primary work as a council. Some of these might be found in Church documents, works of contemporary writers, issues as highlighted in editorial comments of a local newspaper, and books and articles that allow adults to make sense of what is occurring in their daily lives.

It is recommended that this adult formation be included as part of each council meeting and can be accomplished beforehand by asking members to read a certain article before coming to the meeting. It can be accomplished at the end of a meeting by reserving twenty minutes or more for a focused educational discussion that flows from the article.

Several years ago, the concept of the "learning community" was advocated in the business community. Opportunities for growth and learning were created for members from external sources and from each other, all in response to the question: "What do we need in order to grow?"

Education and formation opportunities for councils can also be planned by designating a certain day or time each year for council members to receive ongoing formation in faith and practice. In order for councils to do their job, both the ordained and the laity need appropriate ongoing formation. This should be done together with the assistance of competent outside presenters or facilitators.

In planning the agenda for council meetings, time can be set aside for formative discussion and learning on topics relevant to pastoral life. Leaders can find a wealth of resources in current books, periodicals, and other theological or pastoral publications. This type of ongoing formation within the gathering itself may be preferable to extra gatherings, especially because of time constraints on members.

As he went ashore, he saw a great crowd; and he had compassion for them, because they were like sheep without a shepherd; and he began to teach them many things.

MARK 6:34

Chapter 9

Thomas Augustine Judge, CM
(1868–1933)

The Founder of the Missionary Cenacle Family

It has been said that extraordinary times produce extraordinary people. Looking at the life of Thomas Augustine Judge, CM, one is struck by the character of the man as well as the clarity of mission to which he believed God was calling him.

He lived his life as a faithful son of the Church while remaining true to the inspiration of the Holy Spirit. Periodically, his following of the direction of the Holy Spirit led to confusion or censure by religious authorities. Father Judge continued to seek counsel from those with whom he lived and worked.

~ He was a man who "thought with the Church," not in a robotic sense, but as someone who deeply loved her and constantly sought to understand her thinking and presence in the world.

~ He was persistent in looking at the "signs of the times" to discover the places where God's grace was needed.

~ He remained faithful to an insight given to him as he prepared for ordination. "The idea of a highly spiritualized apostolic laity had been with him since before his ordination, but he did not have a clear picture of just how it might be accomplished or where it might lead." [6]

~ He nurtured this insight with a devotion to the Trinity and especially with a reliance on the Holy Spirit. As he grew in ministry, so did the insight that every baptized person is called to be a missionary within the providence of his or her everyday life. This was a man who well understood the mission field of the ordained and that of the laity.

~ He chose council as a method to bring laity to the table of mission and over time selected it as a method of governance for the two religious congregations founded from within the apostolic laity he formed.

Father Judge was a man ahead of his time. It is difficult for those born after Vatican II to comprehend that he lived in the era when the Church lacked a well developed theology of mission and ministry. Ordained ministry had increasingly become institutionalized, and emphasis was on pastoral authority over pastoral ministry. Ministry was confined to the life and work of the priest. There was no clearly articulated theology of the adult lay Catholic's role either in Church or in society.

Father Judge was ordained a Vincentian priest in 1899. He constantly pondered the issues affecting the lives of the people he pastored. Among those people were the thousands of immigrants coming to this young country from eastern and southern Europe, especially Italians. Many soon left the faith. These immigrants struggled with extreme poverty and the prejudice of those who arrived here before them. He became convinced that he alone could not meet the pastoral needs of the people. His conviction came not only from what he saw, but from what he also believed to be the fundamental mission of the Church. Laity, he believed, had a constitutive place in that mission. This conviction had been with him even before his ordination, and Judge remained steadfast in discerning its meaning.

His spirituality was unusual for the time in which he lived. Born in an era where saving souls was the stated purpose of ministry, Father Judge also believed that each person was the recipient of God's mercy and was to share this with others. He did not believe that the world was evil in itself, but that it was constantly in need of transformation. His spirituality, deemed radical at the time, was ratified later in Vatican II.

Father Judge wanted more than anything to be sent to serve in the foreign missions. Being a missionary in his time meant leaving family and friends and going to far away places where the faith was unknown, to save souls for Jesus. His poor health and other circumstances denied him this privilege of going abroad, but it did not take away his missionary spirit. As a priest, he was not content to care for the people who came only to the rectory. He went out to seek others. He explored the neighborhoods, the work places and streets, the alleys, and even the car barns of his day. He talked easily with all those he met. He discovered that even though the churches were full, there were thousands more who never came under the influence of the Church and were in danger of losing their faith.

He soon realized that he did not need to go far away to be a missionary. He could be a missionary right where he was—in the providence of his everyday life. As a young priest, he pondered the great attrition of Catholics who were being lost to the faith. He made another discovery. It was that every Catholic was called to be good, to do good, and to be a power for good.

This great insight was given to him at a time when bishops, priests, and nuns did all the work, and the layperson was expected to merely obey and help them. He said:

It has been my experience that the people of everyday life are really great missionaries. Looking over a missionary experience of years, I must confess that with the converts who came to me I was but a party to the fact. The first agent in those conversations generally was some man or woman in the office, store or factory.[7]

In 1909, Father Judge met with several women in Brooklyn who were familiar with his thinking through their Vincentian association. He met with them with no premeditated rules or any official name. He feared that too much concern about such things would stifle the Spirit. He simply instructed them to follow the inspirations of the Holy Spirit and to be attentive missionaries to those people and situations they met within their daily providence. This small group grew in size and geography and later became known as the Missionary Cenacle Apostolate.

Something of the attitude of Father Judge is revealed in the following anecdote:

Once when Father Judge was asked by some diocesan officials to explain his work with the laity, he replied that he was teaching lay people to be missionaries, to be responsible for the Church in their everyday lives—in fact, to realize that they are the church. The reaction was immediate and negative: "Father, you can't make missionaries out of lay people." Father Judge's reaction was also immediate: "Pardon me, Fathers, but the lay people are the missionaries. We priests are only a party to the fact; we affirm in a special sacramental way the reconciliation and faith

building that the lay people have begun. Indeed, they are the
real missionaries of the Church.[8]

Where were laypersons to act as missionaries? Father Judge
answered essentially, "wherever your two feet take you."

Over time, Father Judge introduced the "taking of counsel"
into the Cenacle meetings. He would ask the members' advice on
matters of Cenacle development and always sought a greater good.
Following the Vincentian tradition, a structure called "council"
developed, and its purpose was to keep communication open
through the rapidly expanding Cenacles. Everyone was permitted
a voice in the council, although not every thought would be acted
upon. By drawing them into council, Father Judge assured the laity that they were participants in the development of the future of
the Cenacle. He took the laity very seriously. At the same time, he
instructed them that they were to take their own role very seriously
and that they were to pray constantly to the Holy Spirit for guidance and direction. They were also to be prepared beforehand for
the council meeting.

As a faithful son of Saint Vincent de Paul, Father Judge based his
beliefs in the spiritual vision of Vincent. The Vincentian spirit was
rooted in the practice of virtues, which then created a certain type
of character—a missionary. In forming the laity, he encouraged the
practice of distinct virtues for those who wanted to be missionaries
in their daily providence. He did not advocate these virtues for self
centeredness or perfection of the individual. He believed that each
person was to model self on Christ. Daily introspection was to be
performed so that the person would see what was lacking in the
self, what prevented him or her from personal unity with Christ,
and what personal obstacles stood in the way.

The practice of virtue was understood as the manner in which a person sought to eliminate or replace these personal obstacles with the opposite characteristic or virtue. For example, if one saw impatience, the corresponding practice would be in seeking to attain greater patience, even if he or she were to work on this until death. He insisted that all Cenacle members have a practice on which they were to examine themselves daily.

Father Judge believed that the laity needed to be free to work with and search out the abandoned people and issues. They were not to become parish institutions. In Judge's view, the laity spent their time and energy in places where he would never be invited. One could say that Father Judge did not found the Cenacle to do parish work per se. The parish was a place of spiritual nurturance and support. It was the place where people were invited to come home after they had left their faith. It was the role of the missionary to bring them back to church.

Father Judge's insights about the signs of the times were described this way:

> Father Judge...began with the simple statement that "Our Lord would not be fair with us if He did not give us a way of finding out His Will." God has a will for us, a plan, and therefore He certainly will provide us with the means of discovering that will.[9]

How is this will to be discovered? He goes on to say that it is discovered in the teaching of the Church, in the Gospel, and in the voice of circumstances.

He was clear that reading the signs of the times was more than an intellectual analysis of events. To him it was "the need to pray through these events, to allow them to reveal to us the God who is within them and through them."[10]

Father Judge suffered from the suspicion of Church authorities and was sent to Opelika, Alabama, in the hope that this work would cease. Trusting in the Holy Spirit, however, he continued the journey with the laity who followed him.

During this time, a small number of women sought to live a more intentional life of dedication to missionary work within an intentional form of communal living. The outline of a nascent religious community began to emerge. Father Judge soon realized that their mission was the work of the Church. By 1918, they were known as the Missionary Servants of the Most Blessed Trinity. The other men and women continued to live as lay missionaries.

Three men and soon a few others became The Missionary Servants of the Most Holy Trinity, a religious congregation of brothers and priests. Throughout the development of these three groups, there were lay women who took private vows but continued to live within society. In 1964 these women officially received the name of the Blessed Trinity Institute. The Missionary Cenacle Family was born.

Today this family in the Church exists from New England to Florida, throughout the South and the West Coast of the United States, and in Puerto Rico, Mexico, Costa Rica, and Colombia. Its mission is to foster an apostolic spirit in the laity and to encourage laity to see themselves as missionaries in their everyday lives.

In today's era of rapid change, some of Father Judge's concerns still exist. Looking backward can sometimes help us to look forward. Father Judge was a pastorally creative man. He looked around him, saw the suffering of the people, and knew that he could not and should not do pastoral care alone. His genius was in his insight that there were more laity than clergy in the mission of the Church. He gave very little time to writing bylaws or taking management courses. His leadership was revealed in his clarity of mission. He met the laity at the table of council.

Toward the end of his life, Father Judge further developed his understanding of the collaboration that was needed between the lay missionaries and the two religious congregations he had founded. The religious were to keep the laity always in front of their minds. When the laity failed or became disheartened in their missionary focus, Judge was quick to assess that the religious were not fulfilling their responsibility toward them. They were to meet in council together, to share the joys and sorrows of the mission field, and above all, they were to be united in prayer. Council was their place of meeting, praying, and discerning God's will for the Cenacle and its mission.

Today, the Missionary Cenacle Family uses council as the place of sharing their apostolic story, and as a method of governance. The taking of counsel in council is a rich legacy given by a Vincentian priest who believed that laity were the primary missionaries to society.

Your Daily Providence

Make no mistake about it.
We are not talking about the routine of your daily life.
But the providence of your daily life...
What is in the providence of your daily life?
Everything. Absolutely everything.

All the people, the good and the bad.
All the circumstances, the good and the bad.
All the things that happen.
It includes your gifts and your lack of gifts.
Your strengths and your weaknesses,
your health and your energy.
It includes your growing up and your getting old.
It includes your work and your losing your work.

It includes your getting an education and your getting a job.
It includes your making vows of celibacy, your getting
married, your becoming a parent, a grandparent,
        an uncle or aunt.
It includes everything.
In short it is your whole life
        and all the people you come in contact with
is a great and mysterious field of opportunities.

It is yours indeed; it does not belong to anybody else.
Like the skin on your face it is yours personally,
nobody else ever had it,
nobody else ever will have it.
Everyone is a center
        of a particular bit of Divine Providence.
How can we get our people
to realize that in their everyday providence,
they are the Catholic Church,
...can we effect that every Catholic,
        no matter in what circumstances,
he (or she) will be a missionary.

FATHER THOMAS A. JUDGE [11]

Chapter 10

closing Thoughts:
The Church's gift of council

Keep your Church alert in faith
to the signs of the times
and eager to accept the challenge of the gospel.
Open our hearts to the needs of all humanity,
so that sharing their grief and anguish,
their joy and hope,
we may faithfully bring them the good news of salvation
and advance together on the way to your kingdom.

EUCHARISTIC PRAYER
MASSES FOR VARIOUS NEEDS AND OCCASIONS, III

Does the Church have a gift to offer modern society? Rather than adapting the best practices of business or other groups to pastoral life, the Church is called to offer society something deeper in the way it gives and receives counsel.

Today we find councils throughout the United States and around the world. There are councils for wellness, airports, cities, photography, Boy and Girl Scouts, fishery management, students, nursing homes and tree planting—to name only a few. On the global level, we have the United Nations Security Council. The majority of these councils are connected to governance of the organization and they seek to include a variety of people in the process of decision making or planning for the future.

Is it any wonder that Catholics in America have become somewhat cynical if not confused when the Church advocates councils only to "advise" the pastor or leader? If the Church is the people of God, if baptism is the sacrament that initiates all into the universal call to holiness, then why is a pastoral council simply advisory? Why can't it make decisions especially through a simple vote or majority rule? After all, this is what American citizens do in almost every other arena, isn't it?

This book does not shy away from this sensitive issue but rather examines the situation through a new lens. Council in the Church is simply not the same as council in American or world society.

The Church's gift of council to the modern world is seen in at least four realities.

Insights Culled From 2,000 Years of Taking Counsel

The Church did not just recently come up with the great idea of council to sell a product or affect a bottom line. On the contrary, council has been an integral part of the Church's life throughout its history.

A review of literature in recent years demonstrates a growing interest in "taking counsel" in business and education. The title of one article, "Taking Advice: How Leaders Get Good Counsel and

Use It Wisely," by Dan Ciampa, is such an example. He stresses that all humble leaders need constructive counsel obtained through quality listening to others. There is no board of directors in any company today who would disagree with this premise.

Because of the Church's history, it has great wisdom to contribute to this conversation with society.

The Church's Ongoing Efforts at Collaboration in Ministry

The Church has had to engage the challenges of collaboration in modern society within its hierarchical structure. While the word "collaboration" is mainstream today, the Church was already examining itself and its commitment to collaboration in the 1970s. This commitment opened up many different viewpoints and surfaced the struggles of laity and ordained working together within parish and diocesan structures. The work of Loughlan Sofield, ST, and Carol Juliano, SHCJ, was among of the earlier books on the topic of collaboration. Thousands of workshops across the United States and beyond soon followed.

Collaboration takes on another dimension in taking counsel.

~

A pastor related that the lay man he had hired as his pastoral associate had to make the mental shift from working for a company boss to seeing himself as a partner with the pastor. In the parish, his opinion was not only needed but valued. The pastor made it clear that he held an invaluable place in parish life. He possessed distinct gifts that the pastor did not. Even though a hierarchy existed, this did not become an issue for two reasons. The pastor deeply respected the lay man's perspective and experience, and the lay man was willing to work at seeing himself as a partner with the pastor in mission.

~

The gift the Church offers is this very struggle with collaboration. In a hierarchal system, it is easy to fixate on the problems of the "system." Collaboration is possible only to the degree that people (lay and ordained) value each other's field of mission and recognize that they cannot fulfill the Church's mission without the other. The imperative to do this requires a renewed attitude of openness within the ordained and the laity.

Statements of the U.S. Bishops Conference: A Model

It is instructive to review the history of statements made by the United States Catholic Bishops in the past several decades. Some of these documents (*Economic Justice For All; The Challenge of Peace: God's Promise and Our Response*) involved wide consultation among Catholics across the country. Other documents are the result of bishops' committees which included the counsel of experts on the topic at hand. We see contemporary examples of the Church's conciliar process at its very best in these pastoral overtures.

The ongoing preference for such counsel is articulated by Archbishop Timothy Dolan in a 2004 lecture in the Erasmus Lecture series held in New York:

...He [Pope John Paul II] quoted from an array of documents and pastoral letters that the American bishops had issued on spiritual, moral, and pastoral matters; he affirmed their teaching and challenged them to continue and strengthen it; and, in the

process, he shrewdly gave a papal benediction to the genius of the American hierarchy for working collegially, collaboratively, and in concert. It was as if the Successor of St. Peter was nodding in agreement with the observation of James Hennessy, S.J., that "...the bishops of the Catholic Church in the United States have perhaps the proudest conciliar tradition in the Church universal."

Archbishop Dolan continues:

The prelates of this country feel that they need conciliarism, they know that they enjoy it, and they believe that it can be transformed to serve their purposes. All have ideas about how its authority can be better exercised, and the very nature of the collaborative style common to our national ecclesiastical polity since the 1780s will guarantee that current criticism is heeded... it is clear that the conciliar tradition of the American hierarchy is here to stay.[12]

The work of the bishops in addressing current pastoral concerns implicitly involves an immense amount of collaboration with clergy and laity throughout its various departments and in consultations with the People of God. The bishops, as leaders, model the process of taking counsel in their desire to offer pastoral vision and responses to society.

Religious Life and
Emerging Forms of Community

Religious Congregations and Council

Those in consecrated life bring unique gifts to the table of council. Many of these apostolic religious are found in parish work, diocesan offices, social services, and other unique places of ministry. Their experience and life in the Church offers a perspective that is different from the ordained and the laity.

Religious are often not as visible in today's church and society as they were in previous eras. The impact of women religious in the United States before Vatican II was profound. One example of their influence can be seen in the PBS film, *Sisters of Selma*. Another example is in the exhibition that traveled the United States entitled, "Women and Spirit: Catholic Sisters in America."

This does not mean that men and women religious are absent or without influence today. Their voices must be heard and respected as the Church continues to develop its processes of taking counsel.

Over the years, it has been a privilege to work with religious congregations. The type of work has varied, but predominately it has been chapter work. Chapters are a very important time in the life of a religious congregation. How often they occur will vary according to the constitutions or rules of the particular group. Some chapters are held to discern direction for the future, others are held for the selection of leadership. At times these are held separately; at other times together. The charisms and the internal struggles may differ, but the fundamental desire to know and to be faithful to the will of God is universal.

In her research on the early founding of the Daughters of Charity, Margaret Kelly, DC, writes about the methods used by St. Vincent DePaul in establishing councils as a framework for decision making.

As a son of St. Vincent, these very principles would have influenced Father Judge.

The gifts of these congregations and institutes have laid the groundwork for healthcare systems, schools, and social services in this country. These institutions and apostolates were their response to the signs of their times, expressions of their desire to be faithful to God's will, and their formal pastoral responses to the challenges of evangelizing God's people in the new country.

L'Arche and Council

L'Arche is an ecumenical and interfaith community of people, some of whom are mentally and physically handicapped. Founded by Jean Vanier, a Roman Catholic layman in the 1960s, it adopted council as a method of determining its corporate life together.

L'Arche is found in thirty-six countries with over one hundred thirty-five communities. Its mission is deeply connected to mutual relationships of disabled and non-disabled people as they live a form of community life. Together they have a mission to society that is articulated as the desire to transform the society through the witness of this relationship.

L'Arche is a community, as well as a social service agency. The challenge is to keep its core identity as a faith-based community that at times must take government funding. To remain faithful to their founding charism, L'Arche has depended upon the use of counsel supported through discernment. It has also adapted faith sharing and mission reflection as tools to keep it focused on its profound mission.

L'Arche is an example of an emerging form of community because it carries on the age-old tradition of council to discern the signs of the times.

The Church has much to offer society as it learns to use councils, to take counsel, and to operate out of the motivation of virtue not driven by success. The challenge is to find the ways to reflect on human experience, to articulate it, and to offer it in a way that people can hear it in the midst of so many competing voices. Counsel in council is a powerful structure to be used for this ongoing renewal.

The kingdom of heaven is like treasure hidden in a field, which someone found and hid; then in his joy he goes and sells all that he has and buys that field.

Again, the kingdom of heaven is like a merchant in search of fine pearls; on finding one pearl of great value, he went and sold all that he had and bought it.

MATTHEW 13:44–46

Appendix A
Reflective Exercises for Use in Council

On the Role of Counsel

Objective: To deepen the understanding of the role of counsel.
Scripture: Matthew 13:44–46

Questions for Faith Sharing and Mission Reflection

1. Recall personal life experiences in which you sought counsel from others. What effect did this have on your decision?
2. During your time as a member of the group, reflect on the group's history (failures and successes) in giving counsel.
3. What wisdom and understanding does the council have regarding issues in the parish and community that have never been shared?
4. How might these matters be brought to the table of council?

On the Role of Council

Objective: To deepen the understanding of council.
Scripture: Matthew 13:51–52

Questions for Faith Sharing and Mission Reflection

1. What life experiences have trained me for the kingdom of heaven?
2. What is our history as a council? When did it begin, and how has it developed over time?
3. How knowledgeable and current is our council with changes occurring in the wider community?

On Virtue

Objective: To examine the place of virtue in council.
Scripture: Wisdom 7:7–16, Proverbs 2:1–5.

Questions for Faith Sharing and Mission Reflection

1. What virtues have I had to develop because of significant life experiences?
2. What virtues are most operative and most challenging in us as a council?
3. What virtue(s)—or lack thereof—best describe the community we serve?
4. What virtue(s) are most required to serve the needs of this community?

On Our Field of Mission

Scripture: Luke 9:10–11

Questions for Faith Sharing and Mission Reflection

1. What is the mission field of my everyday life?
2. How do we bring the questions, issues, and concerns of our lives to the table of council?
3. How is our pastoral care of the community clarified and implemented through this dialogue in council?

On Becoming a Community of Faith

Scripture: Romans 8

Questions for Faith Sharing and Mission Reflection

1. What qualifications and dispositions do I bring to the table of council?
2. From my experience in council, what spiritual methodologies are most appropriately used? When? Why?
3. As the council develops as a community of faith, how does this affect the community being served?

On Transfiguration or "Change"

Scripture: Mark 9:2–10

Questions for Faith Sharing and Mission Reflection

1. What is the meaning of "transfiguration" in my life at this moment?
2. How is our understanding and practice of council being challenged in light of this passage of Scripture?
3. In what way is this community in need of transfiguration or change?

Appendix B

The Authors

Sister Brenda Hermann, MSBT, ACSW

I do not remember my baptism. Like being born, I was present for the event but not aware of it! Only years later, as I seek to live each day faithful to God's will, have I come to a greater understanding of how the gift of baptism has shaped me.

Early in my youth I was told to be good because God was always watching me—similar to a belief in Santa Claus: "He sees you when you're sleeping, he knows when you're awake, he knows if you've been bad or good, so be good for goodness' sake." I lived with the belief that God's eye was always on me. As I grew older, similar to Santa Claus, this eye of God became more of a myth than a reality. It receded into my awareness but was not the principle for living my life.

As a Missionary Servant of the Most Blessed Trinity, I revisited the image and understanding of the ever-present "eye" of God. Deep in our religious congregation's tradition is the call of the founder to live our lives conscious of God's presence in all things. Everything we see, feel, the people we meet, events, and what we choose to do are all part of this providence.

As this belief unfolds, it lends itself to asking some serious questions. If I am living in God's presence and God's providence is always there, how do I know what choices to make? What is God's will when there are so many options and each one looks better than the other? Rarely am I faced with unequivocal evil. Most of my life's events presented several potentially good choices. What I have needed is the wisdom to know which would be not just good, but better or the best. In my formation as a Missionary Servant of the Most Blessed Trinity, a heavy emphasis was placed on the belief that while God's providence is always there, so is the reality that I share in the providence of others.

My apostolic life has been in diocesan leadership of Catholic Charities, working with organizations across many international cultures, facilitating religious congregations, staffs, clergy groups, and lay communities in different parts of the world. My professional background in social work coupled with my religious congregation's formation has allowed me to work comfortably with groups and systems. However, it does not mean that I am always conscious of the great gift of the counsel of others.

One such incident remains in my memory. I was sent as a director of a Catholic Charities office. One of its services was to provide food and clothing to the poor of the area. After several months, it became clear that this service was used by only a few people who had become regular clients. It was becoming difficult to keep the operation financially sound. So, I made the decision to close the center. However, I neglected to take counsel with the clergy of the deanery. It was a serious mistake, and it took me well over a year to regain their trust in my leadership.

Another memory is about the composite of the multiple pastoral councils with whom I have worked over the last twenty-five years. I have vivid recollections of some of these groups in the early stages of their development and the utter frustration of some pastors about the "nitpicking" (their words) that occurred around decisions where laity's counsel was offered but was really not required. The laity often expressed dissatisfaction in coming into council work, as its focus was so much on plant, property, business, etc. They also were not clear about the meaning of "pastoral work," much less what they were expected to contribute to the conversation. Over the years, the focus has changed and there is more clarity. However, the age-old concern remains: How does a pastor sit at the table in dialogue with his people to receive appropriate counsel? What does the laity contribute from the providence of their everyday life? How are the wisdom of the pastor and the wisdom of the people to be brought together to discern the will of God for the community?

Each of these stories reflects a process of growth within me about the value of counsel within council. My religious congregation, my being a part of a "family" in the Church, and the continued reflections with Monsignor Gaston over these last many years continues to shape my belief in this treasure of the Church. It is needed today.

Monsignor James T. Gaston

My earliest recollection of "receiving counsel" goes back to my formative years in the seminary. There I was introduced to the spiritual life, and over the years, I have sought spiritual counsel from many people who helped me develop a focused spiritual life, a clearer understanding of God, and the ability to search for God's will in my life. Who could make this journey without such support and counsel?

As a pastor and leader in the intervening years, I have learned many times over how much I needed to rely on others' counsel and advice. I have had ample occasions to learn the importance of listening and taking counsel to formulate a response to the pastoral needs of the people in the communities I have served. Each assignment brought with it a unique culture that was new and foreign to me at the outset. How was I to integrate into each environment to minister appropriately?

In my first pastorate—a small, rural parish—I took the suggestion to visit people at home informally and conducted small group gatherings of parishioners in their homes to hear their stories about the past and their hopes for the future. These were wonderful encounters and strategies in that time and place.

In my next pastorate—a much larger, suburban parish—I assumed that I could do the same thing and convene similar listening sessions. I quickly realized this wouldn't work. The people weren't home; they worked! Their culture and concerns were quite different from those of the previous parish. What was I to do now? In place of the earlier intimacy and informality, I discovered anonymity, complexity, and busy-ness in the larger setting. Now what to do? I had to start all over at the drawing board.

During the 1970s and 1980s, parish councils followed diocesan guidelines developed early after Vatican II. They were adaptations of business models intertwined with the language and theology of stewardship. Meetings focused on parish business. Later on in diocesan work, I oversaw and participated in the development of pastoral council guidelines for the Diocese of Greensburg, entitled, *New Wine, New Wineskin*. Its vision and structure, focused on pastoral planning, was a vast improvement and has since been used in many dioceses. Research then suggested that councils should become visioning and planning bodies. It was a step forward.

More than a decade later, however, experience indicates the need for further evolution in the exercise of pastoral leadership. The challenge for pastoral leaders is to learn how to get the best wisdom from the community in making pastoral decisions. Sister Brenda and I have reflected on this issue and have arrived at some major conclusions, the fruit of which is the substance and reason for this book.

We no longer view pastoral councils as the primary planning body in a parish. Planning is not an essential council function; it can be delegated to a staff or to another parish group. In addition, the planning model focuses primarily on the parish, its programs and its activities. Too often this is done while neglecting to ponder the massive changes occurring in the lives of the people, churched and unchurched.

The role of the pastoral council in our emerging view is to refocus the pastor and pastoral leaders on the prior need of understanding the deeper issues buried in the culture in the changing lives of the people being served. Such a vision of council precedes planning.

I am more aware of the need to remain in dialogue with the people I serve. To that degree I can engage them more effectively in pastoral life and authorize pastoral planning that is more relevant. The pastoral council has become the unique place for this dialogue to occur. I need their ability to reflect on the meaning of their family, work and life experiences and how these experiences are reflected in the lives of their fellow parishioners.

Taking counsel in council has become an important step in helping me to be a more focused pastor. As my understanding of the needs of the people increases, I can then work with the pastoral staff (and others who may have that gift) in developing a pastoral plan. Strategic planning can flow from this process, but it must be an intentional response to the "signs of the times" in the lives of the people, not to a theoretical notion of what a parish should be or what I want to do.

It had not occurred to me until recently that in my gathering in council I was continuing in an age-old tradition of the Church. It was comforting to realize that I did not have to come up with something entirely new. I had only to continue using the forum and process followed by many before me in the history of the Church.

Endnotes

1 Pope Paul VI, Decree on the Pastoral Office of Bishops in the Church, *Christus Dominus*, 31. October 28, 1965.

2 Sister Joseph Miriam Blackwell, MSBT. *Ecclesial People: A Study in the Life and Times of Thomas Augustine Judge, C.M.* Philadelphia: Missionary Cenacle Press. Second Edition, 1984. Footnote 539, p. 145. All rights reserved. Used by permission of Missionary Cenacle Press.

3 Jean Marie Hiesberger, *Fostering Leadership Skills in Ministry: A Parish Handbook*, Liguori, MO: Liguori, 2008, 63. Copyright © 2003, 2008 Jean Marie Hiesberger. Used by permission.

4 William Barry, SJ, "Communal Discernment as a Way to Reconciliation," *Human Development*, Vol. 29, no. 3, Fall 2008, 11. Copyright © 2008 Human Development. Used by permission of Regis University, Denver, CO.

5 Shaun McCarthy, ST, "Some Reflections on the Gift of Council and Spiritual Discernment," Unpublished work, 2002. All rights reserved. Used by permission of Missionary Servants of the Most Holy Trinity, Silver Spring, MD.

6 Blackwell, 58.

7 From a compilation of the writings of Father Judge, Philadelphia: MSBT Archives.

8 Blackwell, Footnote 483, 141.

9 Dennis Berry, ST, *God's Valiant Warrior*, Philadelphia: Missionary Cenacle Press, 1992, 284. Copyright © 1992 Missionary Cenacle Press. Used by permission.

10 Berry, 340.

11 From a passage entitled, "Your Daily Providence," a compilation of writings of Father Thomas A. Judge. Copyright © Missionary Cenacle Family. Used by permission of Missionary Cenacle Press, Philadelphia, PA.

12 Timothy Dolan, "The Bishops in Council," *First Things*, April 2005. Copyright © 2005 First Things: A Journal of Religion, Culture, and Public Life. Used by permission of Institute on Religion and Public Life, New York, NY. Available at   http://www.firththings.com/article/2009/04/the-bishops-in-council-1243136062, accessed February 24, 2010.

Bibliography

These resources were consulted in preparing this book or are noted for further reference:

Aquinas, Thomas. *The Commentary of St. Thomas Aquinas on the Book of Job*. Translated by Brian Mullady, OP. Western Dominican Province, 2002. http://www.opwest.org/Archive/2002/Book_of_Job/tajob.htm
———. *The Summa Theologica of St. Thomas Aquinas*. Online Edition. http://www.newadvent.org/summa/.
Arbuckle, Gerald A., SM. *Earthing the Gospel: An Inculturation Handbook for the Pastoral Worker*. Maryknoll, NY: Orbis Books, 1990.
———. *Refounding the Church: Dissent for Leadership*. Homebush NSW Australia: St. Paul Publications-Society of St. Paul, 1993.
Barry, William, SJ. "Communal Discernment as a Way to Reconciliation." *Human Development* 29, 3, Fall 2008.
Berry, Dennis, ST. *God's Valiant Warrior*. Philadelphia, PA: Missionary Cenacle Press, 1992.
Blackwell, Sister Joseph Miriam, MSBT. *Ecclesial People: A Study in the Life and Times of Thomas Augustine Judge, CM*. Philadelphia: Missionary Cenacle Press. Second Edition, 1984.
Brediger, Lawrence, ST. *Sparks of Faith: Selected and Compiled From the Writings of Father Judge, C.M.* Silver Spring, MD: Trinity Missions, 1974.
Carey, Patrick W. *Catholics in America: A History*. Santa Barbara, CA: Praeger, 2004.
Ciampa, Dan. "Taking Advice—How Leaders Get Good Counsel and Use It Wisely." A Harvard Business School Press Book Summary. November 15, 2006.
Coblenz, Stanton A. *Aesop's Fables*. Norwalk, CT: The C.R. Gibson Company, 1968.

Congregation for the Clergy, Instruction. *The Priest, Pastor and Leader of the Parish Community.* Rome: Libreria Editrice Vaticana, August 4, 2002.

Coriden, James A., PhD. *The Parish in Catholic Tradition History, Theology and Canon Law.* Mahwah, NJ: Paulist Press, 1992.

Dolan, Timothy M. "The Bishops in Council." *First Things,* April 2005. Available at http://www.firstthings.com/article/2009/04/the-bishops-in-council-1243136062, accessed February 24, 2010.

Dulles, Avery, SJ. "The Mission of the Laity." L.J. McGinley Lecture. New York: Fordham University, March 29, 2006.

Fiorenza, Joseph A. *Presidential Address.* General Assembly. National Conference of Catholic Bishops. Washington, DC, November 15, 1999.

Fisher, James T. *Catholics in America.* New York, NY: Oxford University Press, 2000.

Flannery, Austin, OP. (Gen. Ed.) *Vatican Council II: Constitutions, Decrees, Declarations.* Northport, NY: Costello Publishing Company, Inc., 1996.

Greeley, Andrew. *The Catholic Revolution: New Wine, Old Wineskins, and the Second Vatican Council.* Berkley, CA: University of California Press, 2004.

Hiesberger, Jean Marie. *Fostering Leadership Skills in Ministry: A Parish Handbook.* Liguori, MO: Liguori, 2008.

Hennesey, James. *The First Council of the Vatican: The American Experience.* New York, NY: Herder and Herder, 1963.

In Fulfillment of Their Mission: The Duties and Tasks of a Roman Catholic Priest: An Assessment Project. Washington, DC: National Catholic Education Association, Seminary Department, 2008.

Jedin, Hubert. *Ecumenical Councils of the Catholic Church: An Historical Survey.* Mahwah, NJ: Paulist Press, 1961.

Keating, Thomas, OCSO. *Fruits and Gifts of the Spirit.* Herndon, VA: Lantern Books, 2000.

Kelly, Margaret J., DC. "Decision Making: Councils of the Daughters of Charity (1646–1659)." *Vincentian Heritage Journal,* Vol. 16, 1, 1995.

Lynch, Donald, ST. *Man On Fire.* Silver Spring, MD: Missionary Servants of the Most Holy Trinity, 1971.

Martini, Carlo Maria, SJ. "Teaching the Faith in a Postmodern World." *America*, May 12, 2008.

McCarthy, Shaun, ST. "Some Reflections on the Gift of Council and Spiritual Discernment," 2002. (Unpublished; written in preparation for the document, *Council: A Tradition of the Missionary Cenacle Family*. Philadelphia: Missionary Cenacle Press, 2003.)

Missionary Cenacle Meditations From the Writings of Father Judge (third printing). Philadelphia: Missionary Cenacle Press, 1972.

Mission Impossible. Paramount Pictures, 1986.

Nerney, Catherine and Hal Taussig. *Re-Imagining Life Together in America: A New Gospel of Community*. Chicago: Sheed and Ward, 2002.

New Wine, New Wineskin: Revisioning the Parish through the Ministry of the Parish Pastoral Council. Diocese of Greensburg, PA, 1996.

O'Bryan, James P., ST. *Awake the Giant*. Philadelphia: Missionary Cenacle Press, 1986.

O'Malley, John W. "Vatican II: A Break From the Past." *Commonweal* 128, March 9, 2001.

Peter, Val J. *Seven Secular Challenges Facing 21st Century Catholics*. Mahwah, NJ: Paulist Press, 2009.

Pieper, Josef. *The Four Cardinal Virtues*. Notre Dame, IN: University of Notre Dame Press, 1966.

Pope Benedict XVI. Encyclical. *Deus Caritas Est*. Rome: Libreria Editrice Vaticana, December 25, 2005. Encyclical. *Caritatis in Veritate*. Rome: Libreria Editrice Vaticana, June 29, 2009.

Pope John Paul II. Apostolic Letter. *Tertio Millennio Adveniente*. Rome: Libreria Editrice Vaticana, November 10, 1994. Post Synodal Exhortation. *Christifideles Laici*. Rome: Libreria Editrice Vaticana, December 30, 1988.

Pope Paul VI, Decree on the Pastoral Office of Bishops in the Church, *Christus Dominus*, 31. October 28, 1965.

Pope Paul VI. Encyclical. *Evangelium Nuntiandi*. Rome: Libreria Editrice Vaticana, December 8, 1975.

Pope Pius XII. Encyclical. *Mystici Corporis*. Rome: Libreria Editrice Vaticana, June 29, 1943.

Rediger, Lawrence, ST. *Sparks of Faith: Selected and Compiled from the Writings of Father Judge, C.M.* Silver Spring, MD: Trinity Missions, 1974.

Rivers, Robert S., CSP. *From Maintenance to Mission: Evangelization and the Revitalization of the Parish.* Mahwah, NJ: Paulist Press, 2005.

Rolheiser, Ronald, OMI. *Secularity and the Gospel: Being Missionaries to Our Children.* New York: Crossroad Publishing Company, 2006.

Second Vatican Council. *Gaudium Et Spes,* Pastoral Constitution on the Church in the Modern World, December 7, 1965.

Sisters of Selma. PBS Home Video, 2007.

Sofield, Loughlan, ST, and Carroll Juliano, SHCJ. *Collaboration: Uniting Our Gifts in Ministry.* Notre Dame, IN: Ave Maria Press, 2000.

Stang, William DD. *Pastoral Theology.* New York, NY: Benzinger Brothers, 1897.

Taking Counsel Together: Council in the Missionary Cenacle Family. Philadelphia: Missionary Cenacle Press, November 23, 2003.

The Mission. USA Warner Brothers, 1986.

United States Conference of Catholic Bishops. Washington DC. *Fulfilled in Your Hearing: The Homily in the Sunday Assembly,* 1982. *Called and Gifted for the Third Millennium,* 1995. *Catechism of the Catholic Church,* Second Edition, 1997. *Everyday Christianity: To Hunger and Thirst for Justice: A Pastoral Reflection on Lay Discipleship for Justice in a New Millennium,* 1999. *Infusing the Pastoral Council with the Spirit of Christ,* Sister Kathleen Turley, RSM, MA, 2004. *Co-Workers in the Vineyard of the Lord,* 2005. *Program of Priestly Formation,* Fifth Edition, 2006.

Witham, Larry. "Film Takes a Catholic Look at Vatican II." *The Washington Times,* September 16, 1998.

Women and Spirit: Catholic Sisters in America. Leadership Conference of Women Religious. http://www.womenandspirit.org/.

Wuthnow, Robert. *After Heaven: Spirituality in America Since the 1950s.* Berkley, CA. University of California Press, 1998.